WHY EVERYTHING IS DIFFERENT ?

Unravelling the nature's complexity through science & Philosophy

DR. ILIYAS HUSSAIN

WHY EVERYTHING IS DIFFERENT ?

Made with ♥ on the Notion Press Platform

www.notionpress.com

DEDICATION

I dedicate this book to my esteemed parents, **Mr. Hamid Hussain** and **Mrs. Sabari Begum,** and my wife, **Dr. Farhana Khatoon.** Their unwavering love, sacrifices, and wisdom have been the foundation of my journey. Their prayers and support have been my greatest source of strength and inspiration.

I also dedicate this book to my dear friend, the late **Dr. Mohd Kasim Saifi,** whose kindness and wisdom will always be remembered. May Allah (SWT) forgive his shortcomings, bless his soul, and grant him the highest place in Jannatul Firdous.

This book is a small tribute to your love, guidance, and inspiration.

'A PHYSICIST LEARNS MORE AND MORE ABOUT LESS AND LESS, UNTIL HE KNOWS EVERYTHING ABOUT NOTHING

WHEREAS

A PHILOSOPHER LEARNS LESS AND LESS ABOUT MORE AND MORE, UNTIL HE KNOWS NOTHING ABOUT EVERYTHING.'

FOREWORD

Life is a beautiful and complex web of diversity. Every living being, from the tiniest microbe to the largest animal, plays a role in maintaining nature's balance. This balance is shaped by evolution, adaptation, and the constant interaction between organisms and their environment. However, with rapid climate change and global warming, this delicate harmony is now at risk. Understanding biodiversity is not just about science—it is about the survival of life itself.

In this insightful book, Dr. Iliyas Hussain, a dedicated researcher and scholar, explores biodiversity from multiple perspectives, blending science, Unani medicine, and philosophy. His work highlights how living things evolve and adapt, how nature maintains balance, and how human actions impact the world.

A unique aspect of this book is its exploration of biodiversity from the Unani perspective. Unani medicine, an ancient system of healing, views biodiversity as an essential part of health and well-being. According to Unani philosophy, all living beings are composed of four elements—earth, water, air, and fire, and their unique mizaj (temperament) determines their nature and interaction with the environment. Just as human health depends on maintaining a balance between these elements, nature also thrives on harmony among its diverse components. The book delves into how the Unani system classifies plants, animals, and minerals based on their temperament, properties, and medicinal uses, demonstrating the deep-rooted connection between biodiversity and holistic well-being.

Dr. Hussain's research bridges the wisdom of ancient traditions with modern science, making this book a valuable resource for students, researchers, and anyone curious about the wonders of life. "Why Everything Is Different ?" is more than a book on biodiversity, it is a journey into the deep connections between life, nature, and human existence.

I am honoured to introduce this remarkable work and encourage every reader to explore its thought-provoking insights.

Prof. Mohd. Zulkifle
Former Head, Department of Kulliyat,
National Institute of Unani Medicine (NIUM),Bangalore
February 19, 2025

PREFACE

The question *'Why is everything different ?'* invites us on a journey to explore the diverse aspects of life and the universe. This book attempts to answer that question by examining life from multiple perspectives, from its origins to its evolution.". It blends both ancient wisdom and modern science to provide a deep understanding of the forces that shape our existence.

We begin by exploring the very essence of life itself. Where did it come from? How did it evolve? What is its purpose? These questions have intrigued philosophers, scientists, and thinkers for centuries, and in this book, we will dive into these mysteries, starting with the beginning of life and its ongoing evolution. We will also discuss how different philosophies, especially those from Elementology, explain life in terms of the basic elements of nature.

The book also looks at the deeper philosophical questions of life and death, encouraging us to think about our existence and its meaning. This is tied together with Unani medicine's perspective on biodiversity, which helps us understand how all living things are interconnected and Interdependent. Another important concept I will explore is the philosophy of equitable temperament, which looks at how nature maintains balance in all things.

I will also discuss how human beings, animals, and plants are all linked in terms of their structure, function, and temperament. This means looking at how our physical and mental states are shaped by the world around us, and how everything is connected through the balance of our internal and external environments.

In this context, I will explain concepts like Kayfiyāt (qualities), Surat (form), and Hayūlā (amorphous substance), which help us understand the nature of matter itself.

This book explores the three main kingdoms of nature minerals, plants, and animals, showing how they are different yet connected. It looks at how life evolves, how organs change over time, and how geography affects human behaviour.

Finally, examines how living things adapt to their environment and the deep connections between biodiversity and nature. Through this book, I hope to offer a simple yet comprehensive view of life, drawing on both science and philosophy to answer why everything is different in this world, yet all these differences are beautifully interconnected. I invite you to join me on this journey of discovery, and to reflect on the diversity of life in all its forms.

Dr. Iliyas hussain

ACKNOWLEDGMENTS

Writing a book is never a solo effort, and I am truly grateful to everyone who has helped me bring ***Why Everything Is Different*** to life.

First, I want to thank Allah for His guidance and strength. Without His blessings, this book would not have been possible.

A huge thank you to my family for their love, patience, and constant support. To my parents, who have always encouraged me to seek knowledge and ask questions. Your belief in me has meant the world, and I am forever grateful.

I also want to thank my teachers and mentors, my Guide **Prof. Mohd Zulkifle Sir** (Ex HoD, Dept. of Kulliyat-e-tibb, National Institute of Unani Medicine, Bangalore), **Dr. Tariq Nadeem Khan Sir**,(Head of the Department of Kulliyat-e-Tibb, NIUM, Bengaluru), **Dr. Wasim Ahmad Sir** (Associate Professor in the Department of Kulliyat-e-Tibb, NIUM, Bengaluru), **Dr. Aijaz Anwar Ansari** Sir (Medical Officer, Burhanpur), **Dr. Sohail Ahmad Sir, Dr. Khurshid Alam Sir, Dr. Ramesh kapadiya Sir** (Burhanpur), **Dr. Ashfaque Ahmad sir** (Burhanpur) Your wisdom, advice, and helpful feedback have been so important in shaping my ideas. I've learned so much from you, and you've inspired me to think more deeply.

Thank you to the many scholars and thinkers whose work helped shape the ideas in this book. Your research and insights laid the foundation for the topics I explore, and I am thankful for your contributions.

To my friends, thank you for your encouragement and for always being there to listen and offer feedback. Your support has made this book stronger, and I appreciate you all.

Lastly, thank you, dear readers. I hope this book makes you think differently about the world and encourages you to see how everything is unique yet connected in its own way.

If you find any mistake or technical error in this book, please let us know. Your feedback is very important and will help us improve the next edition. We appreciate your support in making this book better for everyone.

This book is the result of the help and support I've received from many people. I am deeply grateful to all of you for believing in this project and helping me share it with the world.

Thank you.

PROLOGUE

Exploring the Mystery of Life

Since the beginning of time, people have asked one big question: Why is everything different? Why do living things come in so many shapes and forms, yet follow similar rules? Why do people, animals, and plants grow and change in unique ways, yet remain connected to one another? What unseen forces link everything in the universe?

This book seeks to answer these questions. It explores how life began, why living things are different, and what ancient wisdom and modern science say about these differences. From the teachings of old civilizations to today's scientific discoveries, we will see how variety is not just a feature of life—it is the key to its survival.

One important idea in this book is balance and connection. Everything in nature is different, yet nothing exists alone. Nature does not create differences to separate, but to bring harmony. In Unani medicine, temperament (Mizāj) explains why each person and creature is unique, shaped by their environment and natural elements. In science, evolution shows how life changes over time to survive. In philosophy, different ways of thinking make life rich and meaningful.

But this book is not just about facts—it invites you to see the world in a new way. It challenges old ideas, makes you think deeply, and offers a broad view of life, combining science, medicine, nature, and philosophy.

As you read, get ready for a journey that might change how you understand life. In the grand design of the universe, every difference has a reason, every change has a story, and every living thing has a role in the beautiful dance of existence.

Dr. Iliyas Hussain

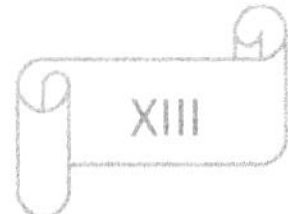

CONTENTS

Chapter 1

About the Life

(origin, Evolution & Existence)

"Live in this world as a traveller, a passerby, with your belongings light and your heart free." — Prophet Muhammad (PBUH)

Life is something everyone knows about and talks about, yet no one has provided a clear, absolute definition of it. Life itself is intangible and non-material, so it doesn't physically exist in the way objects do. Instead, it manifests in bodies, making them "alive." These manifestations, which we call biological functions, include processes like breathing, growing, and reproducing. However, when we ask what "biological" means, the answer is simply that it's something related to or originating from life. The full meaning of life remains a mystery.

Life, on a philosophical level, is a grand question of what it is to be, what our purpose is, and what it is like to exist. Here are some more accessible ways of looking at it from various ideas[61-72]

1-**Existentialism**: This concept is that life does not have a pre-given meaning. Individuals need to discover what their life is about by making decisions and living in a way that is

correct for them. Life will sometimes be confusing or meaningless, yet it is about making your own meaning. [61,62]
2-**Essentialism**: This perspective is that all things, including life, have a purpose or meaning inherent in them. Humans, for instance, may be destined to live a certain way—seeking wisdom or doing good. Life has a natural purpose, and some of living is to find that purpose.[63,64]
3-**Phenomenology**: This perspective is concerned with the way we experience life. It is not merely about being alive, but about how we think and feel about what is around us. Life is something we experience through our senses, thoughts, and feelings, and how we experience life is determined by what happens to us.
4-**Eastern Philosophy**: In the majority of traditions like Buddhism and Hinduism, life is part of a broader cyclical process. Such philosophical viewpoints attend not just to individual lifetime but instead see life as an ongoing process with growth, learning, and finally finding harmony with all of existence. Life is gaining peace and knowing our oneness.
5-**Materialism and Naturalism**: In a scientific view, life is seen as a natural product of chemical and biological processes. Birth, life, and death processes are controlled by physical laws. No deep or mysterious purpose is assigned to life; instead, it is a set of processes taking place in the natural world.
6-**Religious Views**: Most religious traditions view life as a given gift or creation of the supreme god. Life is living

according to a predestined plan or purpose, such as serving a god, being kind to others, or getting ready for an afterlife in the next existence. The purpose of life is closely tied to a higher power or divine plan.

Lastly, the question of "**What is life**" is whether life has a deep purpose or whether it is all about making sense of everyday life, exercising personal freedom, and discovering individual purpose.

Theories of the origin of life attempt to explain how life originally came to be on Earth. While an absolute answer is elusive, many theories have been proposed by scientists and philosophers throughout history. Some of the most notable theories are as follows:

1-**Primordial Soup (Abiogenesis):** This theory requires that life evolved from some basic chemical compounds in the ancient oceans of the Earth. It states that the early Earth conditions (with a mixture of gases, temperatures, and electricity like lightning) triggered chemical reactions that led to the formation of complex molecules resulting in the emergence of the first living organisms. The famous Miller-Urey experiment in the 1950s confirmed this by showing that amino acids (building blocks of life) can be formed under conditions simulating ancient Earth.

2-**Hydrothermal Vent Hypothesis**: This theory suggests that life may have started near deep-sea hydrothermal vents, where heated water rich in minerals rises from the Earth's crust. These vents provide the right conditions for the formation of life, with a supply of chemicals and energy. It's believed that the early forms of life could have been based on the reactions occurring around these vents, which could have provided energy to drive the formation of organic molecules.

3-**Panspermia**: The panspermia theory proposes that life didn't necessarily originate on Earth but was brought here from outer space, carried on comets, meteoroids, or cosmic dust. It suggests that life could exist elsewhere in the universe and that microscopic life forms, like bacteria, might have travelled through space and seeded Earth with life.

4-**RNA World Hypothesis**: This theory suggests that RNA (a molecule similar to DNA) could have been the first genetic material, playing a central role in the origin of life. In this model, RNA molecules may have both stored genetic information and catalysed chemical reactions, allowing early life forms to evolve. Over time, these RNA molecules could have evolved into more complex molecules, including DNA and proteins.

5-**Clay Hypothesis**: Some scientists propose that life might have begun on the surface of clay minerals. These minerals have properties that can help molecules stick together and form more complex structures. The idea is that simple organic molecules could have been catalysed by clay particles, eventually leading to the first living cells.

6-**Deep-Sea Alkaline Hydrothermal Vent Hypothesis**: This is a variation of the hydrothermal vent theory, but it

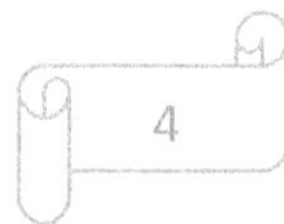

emphasizes alkaline (basic) environments. It suggests that life may have originated in these environments, which are rich in both energy and chemicals that could drive the formation of organic molecules, offering the perfect setting for life to begin.

Before the 750 years of Darwin, Abu al-Hasan Nizam al-Din Ahmad bin Umar bin Ali Samarkandi, known as "**Nizami Aruzi**," was one of the distinguished scholars of the sixth century Hijri. In his work **"Chahar Maqala"** (Four Discourses), he discusses a theory resembling evolution. Nizami Arusi, in his book *Chahar Maqala*, explains the origin of life and the structure of the universe. He describes the world as existing within a hollow sphere inside the **heaven of the moon**. This world is called **"Alem-e-Kaun wa Fasad,"** meaning **"The World of Growth and Decay,"** because everything in it changes over time—things are born, grow, and eventually die.[13]

The universe, according to this explanation, is made up of different layers. The **outermost layer inside the moon's sphere contains fire**. Below this fire is a layer of **air**, then **water**, and at the centre is **the Earth, which is surrounded by water**. At the very middle of the Earth is an **imaginary central point**, which is considered the lowest part of the universe. Surrounding all these layers are **nine celestial spheres**, including the paths of stars, planets, the moon, and the sun.[13]

Nizami Arusi believed that **God created life through the influence of celestial bodies, especially the sun and moon**. These heavenly bodies **control the cycle of growth and decay**. The **sun's heat plays an important role** because it warms things and pulls them upwards. Over time, as the **sun heated the water on Earth**, large amounts of water **evaporated into the sky**, making parts of the Earth's surface dry up and become land.[13]

As this process continued, **mountains were formed** due to the sun's heat. This made the Earth rise slightly, while the water **retreated and dried up**, making land more stable. This new dry land was called the **"Uncovered Quarter"** because it was previously covered by water. It was also called the **"Inhabited Quarter"** because animals and humans began to live there.

As the **stars and planets continued to affect the natural elements**, they helped create various **natural phenomena**. These include mountains, mines, clouds, rain, thunder, lightning, comets, meteors, earthquakes, and springs. These effects result from the interaction between **earth, water, fire, and air**, guided by the stars and celestial cycles.

Once the natural environment had **matured and become stable**, it was time for **plant life to emerge**. God created **special forces** within plants that allowed them to **grow, survive, and reproduce**. These forces include:[13]

1. **The Force of Attraction (Jadhiba):** Plants pull in nutrients from the soil and air.

2. **The Force of Retention (Masika):** Plants hold onto the absorbed nutrients.
3. **The Force of Assimilation (Hadima):** Plants process and change the nutrients into useful substances.
4. **The Force of Expulsion (Dafi'a):** Plants remove unnecessary or harmful substances.

Additionally, plants have a **Reproductive Faculty (Quwwat-i-Muwallida)**, which allows them to **produce seeds** and ensure their species continue to exist. This **ability to reproduce** makes plants more advanced than lifeless minerals and connects them to the next stage of life: **animals**.

Over time, life continued to evolve. The first material of the **mineral kingdom**, which was **clay**, gradually developed and became **coral**, which is the highest stage of minerals. Coral serves as a connection between minerals and plants. In the **plant kingdom**, the simplest plant is the **thorn**, while the most advanced plants are the **date palm and the grapevine**. These plants show characteristics similar to animals:[13]

- The **date palm** needs a **male tree** to fertilize it and bear fruit, just like animals need reproduction.
- The **grapevine** actively **avoids its enemy, the bindweed**, which harms it by wrapping around it and making it wither.

Because of these traits, the **date palm and grapevine** are considered the most developed plants, as they have started to show qualities similar to animals.

Nizami Arusi explains that the **four elements—earth, water, air, and fire—create three interspaces**. These interspaces give rise to three major forms of life, called **"threefold offspring"**:[13]

1. **The Mineral Kingdom** (rocks, metals, and mountains).
2. **The Plant Kingdom** (trees, flowers, and crops).
3. **The Animal Kingdom** (animals and humans).

Each of these life forms is connected, evolving gradually from simple to complex forms, shaping the world we see today.

These theories try to answer the question of how life began, but there's still a lot of research to be done, and it's possible that the true origin of life could involve a combination of these ideas or something completely different.

There are also many theories about the origin of life, but most focus on the evolution or combination of living bodies. One scientific explanation comes from Unani philosophers, who proposed the concept of Elements. According to this idea, living bodies are created from four basic and simple components. These components interact to form complex bodies with a specific ***Mizāj*** (temperament), which is evenly distributed throughout the body.

Mizāj (temperament), along with *Ṭabī'at* (nature) and related abilities, prepares the body to accept life. Life, like other abstract qualities, exists only within a material body and cannot exist on its own. Though it is intangible, life causes the living actions we observe in various parts of the body. [1]

However, it's nearly impossible to establish a clear cause-and-effect relationship between life and these actions. For example, we cannot say for certain whether the heart's beating is life itself or if it beats because of life. Additionally, many forms of life exist without a heart or vital organs. Biological functions are simply expressions of life, sustained continuously by its presence.

When life ends, even a perfectly intact body can no longer perform any living activity. This suggests that life is the driving force behind biological activities, not their result. If life were just an effect, humans could create eternal life artificially—but that's not possible. While a heartbeat and blood circulation can be maintained with machines, they do not constitute life itself. Life is more than these functions, as it exists in many forms, some similar and others different.

The actions and processes associated with life, like movement, breathing, digestion, reproduction, growth, perception, emotions, and thinking, are signs of life but are not life itself. These functions are seen in more complex forms of life but are simply its manifestations, not its essence.

It is not necessary that in all forms of life above mentioned properties and manifestation must be present. In the easiest way, life is comprehended as the continuation of living process and manifestation in any body. From these manifestations some are of higher degree and are associated with developed higher forms of life, others are ubiquitous and present in both the simplest to the most complex form of life. That is why vegetative functions are common in all forms of life including plants. "Therefore, plants are considered living.". [3]

As earlier has been clarified that life does not exist in isolation because it is non-materialistic or non-corporal, hence it always exists in corporeal thing making them animate. Because of this limitation, life can be defined indirectly as "the corporeal body which manifests living task and process is called as having life. For believer and even for non-believer, because its comprehension is beyond the intellect of human beings. Like various forms of energy, life is sensible and can be sensed from external as well as internal senses.

Life can be seen, heard, felt, and thought about, but it cannot be touched. What we touch is only the body that carries life, not life itself. Unlike mechanical processes, where matter is consumed or lost, life is a unique form of energy. It enables growth for a specific period while the body, made of physical matter, follows natural laws. During life, the body experiences both noticeable and subtle losses of matter—for example, through activities like breathing, sweating, or cell turnover.

Life powers various biological functions, such as movement, respiration, digestion, and reproduction, through specific structures like organs and tissues. Beyond these functions, life has another critical role: maintaining the structure and organization of the body. It ensures that the body remains intact and functional. However, once life is lost, this organization breaks down, and the body begins to disintegrate.

According to Unani philosophy, the body is composed of four basic elements (constituents) combined in different proportions. These elements create the physical foundation for life to manifest and sustain the body. Life, therefore, acts as the force that drives the body's growth, functions, and unity, holding everything together until it inevitably fades.

These constituents are called *Element* and these are of opposite as well as similar properties. All the corporeal bodies are made from these *Element*. Amalgamation of differing proportion of *Element* gives rise to different corporeal forms. Because of opposing properties, *Element* tend to get apart from corporeal things; hence, a force is necessary to keep them in association for the integrity of body. [5,6,7,8] During living processes and tasks dissolution, occur. [9] This is inevitable and for continuation and sustenance, loss must be replenished. Obviously, the replenishing material should be identical to the lost one, so that it can be incorporated.

Living organisms require continuous energy to perform their functions. The materials inside the body that generate this energy must also be replenished regularly. This means that for life to continue, the body needs a constant supply of both energy and the materials that are lost during daily activities. Without this, the body would disintegrate, and life would cease.

The body is made from four basic *Elements*, which are used during living processes. These *Elements* are lost through actions like digestion, movement, and growth. To keep the body functioning, the lost materials must be replaced in a form that the body can use. This replenishment happens through food, which is made up of the same four *Elements*.

Food not only sustains life but also supports growth in plants, animals, and humans. The materials in food are burned within the body to release energy, which is used for various biological processes. However, when the body uses more of certain *Elements* than it replaces, it creates a "debt" in those *Elements*. This debt can be tolerated up to a certain point, but if it exceeds a limit, it can cause serious health issues.

In food, the two *Elements* called *Rukn Mā* (Water) and *Rukn Ard* (Earth) dominate. These are energy-deficient and tend to be "cold" in nature, which is why they are less effective in providing energy compared to other *Elements*.

Inside the body, part of the food we eat is "burned" (or metabolized) to produce energy. This burning process causes the *Elements* Air (Hawā') and Water (Mā) to break down and evaporate more quickly because heat naturally causes things to dissolve and become lighter.

As the body uses energy for various tasks, it loses Air (Hawā') and Water (Mā) in excess. These *Elements* are consumed in the energy-producing processes, and over time, the body becomes deficient in them. Diet alone cannot fully replace these lost *Elements*, so extra replenishment is needed. This shows that during life, energy is constantly used for different activities. Since no biological process is perfectly efficient, some energy is always lost in the form of heat.

Energy inside the body is always converted from one form to another but never truly lost. This happens during various processes in the body, like building (anabolic) and breaking down (catabolic) substances. Every time a chemical reaction happens or a task is performed, energy flows from one place to another, and some matter is lost in the process.

As the body continues its tasks, material is constantly lost. Eventually, this loss could deplete the body's material, and since life cannot exist without a body, life would end when all the material is gone. Therefore, the body needs to continuously replenish its material to sustain life.

The four basic *Elements* are the main building blocks of the body, and they are lost during life's processes. To maintain life, these *Elements* must be replenished. As a final analysis it can be said that *Four element* are essential and are playing a crucial and pivotal role in continuation and sustenance of body and there by life.

The Unani System of Medicine is based on philosophical insights and scientific principles, including the theory of four Elements (Fire, Air, Water, and Earth) and four qualities (hot, cold, dry, and wet) described by Pythagoras.[1,16,40]

In the Unani system of medicine, elements are considered indivisible matters that form the primary components of the body. These elements cannot be divided into simpler entities with different forms or functions. All substances in nature exist due to their chemical combination, known as *Imtizaaj (Mixture).1*

The universe is composed of four elements in varying amounts and proportions. Classical Unani literature refers to these elements by various terms, such as *Anāṣir*, *Ustuqussāt*, and *Asl*. While these terms have subtle differences in meaning, they broadly convey the same concept.1

The concept of *Anāṣir* (elements) and their quantities, interactions, and mutual attractions result in *Ṣūrat-e-Mizāji* (temperament), which influences health. *Kayfiyāt* (qualities), being abstract, exist in association with the body. This likely led ancient philosopher to propose four fundamentals elements in nature, corresponding to the qualities found in bodily fluids (*Akhlāṭ*), organs, and diseases.

There are four primary qualities: hot, cold, wet, and dry. Hot and cold are active and oppositional, while wet and dry are passive and oppositional. Each element combines two of these qualities:

- Hot and dry: Fire, Hot and wet: Air
- Cold and dry: Earth, Cold and wet: Water

Ancient philosophers' concept of elements differed significantly from the modern chemical understanding. Their elements symbolized fundamental qualities by which all objects and phenomena are perceived through the senses (e.g., air is felt through touch). Modern science misinterpreted this concept, criticizing it as unscientific and limited to four elements, whereas it was a framework for generalizing qualities in nature.

The Unani System of Medicine views elements as touch-based modalities, generalized into four qualities: heat, cold, dryness, and moisture. These qualities are perceived through touch, either alone or in combination.

Aristotle identified heat and cold as active, representing energy's opposing movements, while moistness (*Ruṭūbat*) and dryness (*Yubūsat*) represent opposing material qualities, unified in temperament (*Mizāj*). According to Ibn Sina, heat and cold actively integrate and transform, while dryness and moisture are passive, being acted upon. Integration is seen as an active process, whereas changes in dryness or moisture occur passively.

Modern science distinguishes mass (chemical components) from energy (photons and waves). In contrast, Unani Medicine relates energy to heat and cold and mass to dryness and moisture:

- Heat: Causes warmth, melting, evaporation, and disintegration.
- Cold: Cools, integrates, freezes, and extinguishes heat.
- Moisture: Softens, smooths, and creates fluidity.
- Dryness: Hardens, stabilizes, and densifies.

From this discussion, it is evident that heat and cold represent opposing directions of energy in space, while dryness and moisture signify contrasting reactions of mass over time. Einstein's principle reinforces this idea, stating that energy and mass are inseparable—everything exists through their simultaneous interaction.

Heat and cold, like dryness and moisture, coexist with varying degrees, ensuring the simultaneous presence of mass and energy qualities. Similarly, the coexistence of motion and rest cannot be fully explained by materialistic chemistry or measurable time.

The Unani System of Medicine uses the symbolic elements of Earth, Water, Air, and Fire to represent this structure. These elements reflect a balance where pure energy exists at its extreme, with primordial time and movement present in minimal proportions. This framework acknowledges the interdependence of mass, energy, time, and motion.

Ibn Sina explained that in living things and *Anāṣir* (elements), the qualities of heat, cold, moisture (*Ruṭūbat*), and dryness (*Yubūsat*) exist in relation to space and time. In the organization of *Anāṣir*, these qualities can show absolute excess or deficiency:

- Heat: Found in Fire and Air
- Cold: Found in Earth and Water
- Dryness: Found in Fire and Earth
- Moisture: Found in Water and Air

Each *Unṣur* (element) shares similarities with higher or lower elements while differing in other properties. These similarities and differences drive interaction among the *Anāṣir*. They maintain individuality through differences while organizing through similarities.

Compounds formed from *Anāṣir* exhibit a dominant property, identified by measuring the proportions of the four qualities. In any compound, these qualities are never entirely absent nor equally balanced, resulting in the dominance of specific traits. Based on this dominance, compounds are classified as fiery (*Nāri*), airy (*Hawā'i*), watery (*Mā'*), or earthy (*Arḍi*).

Life, like qualities such as whiteness or blackness, is an abstract concept that always exists in association with a body, not independently. It is called *'Ard* because it occurs in relation to something else. Health and disease are also *'Ard*, as they are linked to a living body. Therefore, life itself is an abstract quality that is always present with a body, distinguishing between living and non-living things.

Living organisms share several key characteristics:

1. **Order**: Living things have complex structures, starting from simple elements like fire, air, water, and earth. These elements combine to form biomolecules (e.g., amino acids, proteins), which then form organelles and, eventually, the body.
2. **Sensitivity**: Organisms respond to stimuli. For example, plants bend toward light, and bacteria move toward or away from chemicals or light (chemotaxis, phototaxis). Positive responses are movements toward stimuli, and negative responses are movements away.
3. **Reproduction**: Life comes from life. Animals and plants have the ability to reproduce, ensuring the survival of species and the continuity of life.
4. **Growth and Development**: Growth refers to an increase in size, while development is the process of transformation from a single cell to a complex organism. Organisms grow and develop through coordinated processes (e.g., cells, organs, and the human body).
5. **Regulation and Homeostasis**: Organisms have the ability to regulate their internal functions, maintaining balance and coordination within the

body. This ensures optimal conditions for bodily functions and health.

6. **Energy Processing**: Organisms use energy to function. Plants capture solar energy to produce food, while animals obtain energy by consuming food. Energy is used to carry out necessary work within the body.

Here are some different perspectives on life from various authors:

1. **Albert Camus** – He thought life is pointless and confusing, but we should still live fully and find our own meaning.
2. **Friedrich Nietzsche** – He believed life is about overcoming challenges and creating our own path and values.
3. **Leo Tolstoy** – He saw life as a journey to become better people by connecting to a higher power and showing love and kindness.
4. **Erich Fromm** – Fromm thought life is about freedom, love, and finding meaning through relationships and work.
5. **William Shakespeare** – He compared life to a play, where people take on different roles at different stages of life, and we play our parts until the end.
6. **Herman Hesse** – Hesse saw life as a journey to understand ourselves better and grow spiritually.

7. **Mahatma Gandhi** – Gandhi thought life was about serving others, finding truth, and living peacefully with love and fairness.
8. **Jean-Paul Sartre** – Sartre believed life is about freedom and that we must create our own meaning through the choices we make.

Each author gives a different idea of life, but they all agree that life involves personal growth, meaning, and choices.

Chapter 2

Basic constituents of Life

"Everything in the universe has a purpose, even the smallest creature." — Al-Ghazali

---

- **In Unani system of medicine two terms have been mainly used for basic constituents, *Ustuqussāt* and *Arkān*. *Ustuqussāt* is a roman word. Literally it means primary components or substances from which all three creatures (*Nabātat, Haiwanāt*, and *Jamādat*) are made.**

The primordial constituents in the natural world are four i.e. earth, water, air and fire. These are called as primary substances because they are not made of others substances except themselves. Contrary to this, all entities in nature are made of these substances either directly or indirectly. For example, human body which is made up of homogenous organs. Each of them is made first from *Mani* (semen) and thereafter obtains nutrition from *Dam* (blood). *Dam* (blood) is formed from food which comes from animals or plant. The condition of the body of animal resembles the human body. These bodies are formed from plants, and plants are made of earth, water, air and fire. [1]

From the above stanza, it is apparent that *Arkan* is the constituents or matter/substance, and they are *Baseet* (simple). Greek philosopher as stated above, have defined simple in as *Arkān* "whose components do not differ in form, characteristics and properties but have a uniform status". According to modern definition, *Arkān* is a substance which can't be chemically separated into such ingredients whose forms and *Kayfiyāt* (properties) are different from one another. [(12)]

There are a number of individuals who have taken the *Arkān Arba'a* and used them to explain, clarify, or categorize various aspects of the universe and our human experience of it, as well as ourselves. In ancient *Greek* we find the first philosophers who proposed individual *Arkān* is the basic principle/component of the universe.

Theory of one *Arkān*: The continuation of life on Earth has been a topic of debate for both ancient and modern scholars. Various ancient thinkers proposed different theories:

- **Thales** (640-546 BC) and **Hippon** believed that Water (Mā) was the fundamental element from which all things originated. They suggested that the Earth floats on water and that moisture and warmth sustain life, with all seeds having a moist temperament.[6,16,43]
- **Anaximander** (611-544 BC) and Diogenes argued that Air (Hawā') was the origin of all life. They believed air is eternal and, through condensation, transforms into water, earth, or fire.[16,42]

- **Heraclitus**(540-475 BC) proposed that Fire (Nār) was the primary element responsible for the creation of the world, suggesting it was different from the other elements like water, air, and earth.[16,41,42]
- **Jalinus** rejected the idea of life originating from a single element. He argued that at least two basic elements—one active and one passive—are needed to form a compound, resulting in a body with a specific *Mizāj* (temperament). Hippocrates also agreed, stating that if humans were formed from only one element, they wouldn't experience pain, and diseases would require only one type of treatment.

Theory of two *Arkān* : *Arḍ* (earth) and *Mā* (water): . **Xenophanes** (570-470 BC) and some other philosopher advocated that the *Arḍ* (earth) and *Mā* (water) are primordial constituents of *Mawālīd-e-Thalatha.* They stated that to create forms in compounds both moistness and dryness were necessary. As moistness easily accepts various forms and in the same way gives them up, while dryness was necessary to protect the form. This showed that the formation of a compound entirely depends on moistness and dryness, and this purpose could be served by *Arkān* like *Arḍ* (earth) and *Mā* (water). The *Hawā* (air) was a vapor created from *Mā* (water) and it becomes *Nār* (fire) due to the production of *Ḥarārat* (heat) by extreme movement in *Hawā* (air).[(22,23)]

Nār (Fire) and *Arḍ* (earth): Some philosophers thought that *Nār* (fire) and *Arḍ* (earth) are primordial constituents of cosmos. In support of their belief, they gave theory that when compounds dissolved, they normally returned into these two *Arkān*, *Nār* (fire) and *Arḍ* (earth). Air and water were altered forms of *Nār* (fire) and *Arḍ* (earth). Air was like an extinguished *Nār* (fire) which became somewhat *Kaseef* (thickened) because of the vapours released from water, water was melted *Arḍ* (earth); it was lighter than *Arḍ* (earth) due to its mixture with *Nār* (fire).[1,22,23]

However, the two-element theory also failed to fully explain life. This led to the introduction of a three-element concept, categorizing matter into solid, liquid, and gas:

- Solid matter: Rukn Jamida
- Liquid matter: Rukn Water (Māiyya)
- Gaseous matter: Rukn Air (Hawā'iyya)

The theory of three *Arkān*: According to *Ahl-e-Ikseer* or Chemiyadan, a group of philosophers, mentioned that all matters found in this universe are present in three states viz. solid, liquid and gas. They further categorized solid matter as *Rukn Jamida*, liquid matters as *Rukn Mā'iyya* and gaseous matter as *Rukn Hawā'iyya*. They used different terms in their own language for these matters. *Rukn Hawā'iyya* was known as *Kibreet*, *Rukn Mā'iyya* as *Zaibaq* and *Rukn Jamida* was as *Muleh*.[1,22,23]

The theory of *Arkān Arba'a*: The proposer of the theory of *Arkān Arba'a* was a Greek philosophers Empedocles (490-430 BC). Who thought that all matter were composed of a combination of four primordial constituents, viz. earth, water, air and fire. Each of these was ever-lasting but they could be mixed in different proportion, and this produced different complex substances that were found in the universe.[1,2,3,12,16,23,24] His very important theory was love and strife. The aforesaid substances combined by love and are separated by strife. The changes in the cosmos are not governed by any purpose but only by chance and necessity. There was a cycle: when the *Arkān* got thoroughly mixed by love, strife gradually separated them again; when separation completely occurred by strife, love gradually reunited them. Thus, it was assumed by Empedocles that every compound was temporary; only the *Arkān* together with love and strife were ever-lasting. one of the eminent physicians of Unani system in his treatise stated.

It was **Aristotle** who, a century later, extended this doctrine that the *Arkān Arba'a* are primordial constituents of cosmos. According to him earth, water, air and fire were not absolute components of matter; they could be transformed into one another. The properties combined in pair were the mutable, natural and fundamental *Kayfiyāt* (qualities) of matter. According to Aristotle, fire was hot and dry; air was hot and moist; water was cold and moist and earth was cold and dry.[16]They can be seen over the course of the year in the seasons, and are therefore directly and intimately related to the process of growth and decay, i.e. transformation of a cyclic nature. Growth begins in the spring under the influence of moisture, ascends to the warmth of summer, moves into the dryness of autumn, and descends into the coldness of the winter. This is the most noticeable basis for consideration that the *Arkān* manifest through an ordered, cyclic process, from earth to water to air to fire and finally back to earth[(16)].

Aristotle also recognized a fifth essence, the "quintessence", calling it the "aether", of which the heavens were made. According to Aristotle, the aether, was a substance completely different from the four "sublunary" *Arkān* (elements); it was incorruptible, unchanging and everlasting. It moved only in perfect spherical rotation and made up of the heavenly bodies (the moon was made of aether trained by the *Arkān Arba'a*) the fifth element was linked to absolutely non material phenomena, and corresponds to the *Ayurvedic* concept of "*Akash.*" [(7)]

Through Aristotle wide ranging influence, the *Arkān Arba'a* became one of the foundational modes of understanding the manifested world.

The present-day life is based on organic molecules made up of from the atoms of carbon, hydrogen, oxygen, nitrogen, sulphur and phosphorus. However, primitive chemical information may have been started in mineral crystals; this idea has been developed by Cairn-Smith at the University of Glasgow. According to this theory, some clay offered a potential for genetic information in the intrinsic pattern of crystal defects. These clays proliferated and their replicating defects become more abundant.

The hypothesis that if life exists on other planets or moons, it will be carbon based and dependent on water, it will also be self-replicating and capable of evolving. Carbon is the best element for creating macromolecules; it can form chemical bonds with many others atoms to produce biochemical complexity. This complexity consists of thousands of catalytic and structure's proteins and nucleic acid, the informational macromolecules involve in protein synthesis. [(131)]

So, **Empedocles** (490-430 BC) proposed the four-element theory, suggesting that Fire, Air, Water, and Earth were the core elements for the continuation of life. Philosophers like **Hippocrates**, **Aristotle**, and **Plato** adopted this theory, defining these elements as the basic building blocks of life.[16]

In contrast, **Democritus** and his followers proposed an infinite number of elements but could not identify them or explain their role in life's continuation. Their theory did not effectively address the question of life's origin and persistence.

These theories highlight the varying views on what drives the existence and continuation of life.

The four-element theory explains the role of the four elements—Earth (Arḍ), Water (Mā), Fire (Nār), and Air (Hawā')—in the continuation and existence of life. Jalinoos (Galen) provided two arguments to prove the presence of these elements in humans.

Physical Characteristics:

- **Bones**: Hardness, dryness, and coldness suggest the presence of Earth (Arḍ).

- **Phlegm (Balgham)**: Cold and moist qualities indicate Water (Mā).
- **Body Heat:** The warmth of the body points to the presence of Fire (Nār).
- **Air**: The sensation of air indicates the presence of Air (Hawā').

2. **Nutritional Argument:** Humans, like other organisms, receive nourishment from all four elements. For example, if a tree grows and doubles in size, the increase in length is due to the nutrition it receives from the four elements. This shows that the elements in the body are also present in the nutrition, supporting the idea that the same elements sustain life and growth.

Regarding the definition of elements, it's clear that the "elements" used in these theories are simpler and indivisible from a functional or involvement perspective, not necessarily from a material standpoint. For example, calcium oxide (CaO), though a compound, serves as the elemental substrate in a reaction to form calcium hydroxide. While CaO is not indivisible in a material sense, it is considered indivisible in the context of the synthesis process. In the biological world, biomolecules act as substrates for the synthesis of other biomolecules. While these biomolecules appear simple and indivisible in biological processes, they can be broken down into simpler elements like carbon, hydrogen, and oxygen when analysed chemically.

Rukn-e-Ard (Earth)

Phrekides 570-480 BC stated that the earth is a resting place for all things of the universe; if a physical body is detached from its resting place ultimately, it would return to the earth. He believed on this observation that primary *Rukn* was the earth. [12,15,16,17]

Rukn-e-Arḍ (Earth) is considered a simple, heavy matter at the centre of the universe, with a tendency to remain stationary and return to its natural position when displaced. Its qualities are cold and dry, and it is essential for making things hard, firm, and stationary. Earth contains most minerals, which are also found in water and air but in lesser amounts. These minerals are vital for plants and animals because of their ability to rearrange and integrate into living organisms.

Unani physicians believe that when the four elements—Fire (Nār), Air (Hawā'), Water (Mā), and Earth (Arḍ)—combine, they create all substances. If a compound has a dominant presence of water and earth, plants are formed. Plants cannot move because of the dominance of earth and water, but they get nutrients from the earth, water, and air. When air and fire join with earth and water, animals are formed, giving them the ability to move.

Jalinoos (Galen) suggested that plants arise from the primary combination of the four elements, while animals are created through a secondary arrangement. Plants need the four elements—sunlight (energy), air (CO2), water, and earth (minerals)—to survive and become food for animals.

Animals, whether herbivores or carnivores, derive their nutrition from plants or other animals. After death, plants and animals break down into these primordial elements, continuing the cycle of life.

Everything in the world is either an element or a combination of elements. Many mineral elements exist in nature, but only a few are present in the human body. These elements can be categorized into four groups:

1. Major Elements (about 90% of the body): Carbon, Hydrogen, Oxygen, and Nitrogen. These are obtained from dietary fats, carbohydrates, proteins, air, and water.
2. Macro-Elements: Calcium, Phosphorus, Magnesium, Sodium, Potassium, Chloride, and Sulphur. These are required in relatively larger amounts in the diet.
3. Trace Elements: Chromium, Cobalt, Copper, Iodine, Iron, Manganese, Molybdenum, Selenium, and Zinc. These are needed in smaller amounts in the diet.
4. Elements with Undefined Essential Functions in Humans: Arsenic, Cadmium, Nickel, Silicon, Tin, and Vanadium. These have known roles in animals but do not have essential functions in the human body.

Rukn-e-Mā (Water)[110]

Thales 640-546 BC held the view that water was the only primary *Rukn* and the other *Rukn*, viz. *Arḍ* (earth), *Hawā* (air), *Nār* (fire) are the transformed forms of *Mā* (water). He advocated that only the thing which possess the ability to convert easily into different shapes, could assume the status of *Rukn*; Water possesses all those qualities which a thing requires to acquire different forms viz. mobility, wetness, liquidity and coldness; therefore, water should have the status of the primary *Rukn*. Water turns into earth when it condenses and changes into air and fire when it becomes lighter and spreads out.[(1,16,)]

Water is a simple yet essential substance that plays a crucial role in sustaining life. In its natural state, water surrounds the Earth and exists beneath the air. It is heavier than air and fire but lighter than earth. From a temperamentally perspective, water is naturally cold and moist. Its moist nature allows it to spread and take different shapes easily. This flexibility makes water essential for shaping and expanding natural things. Unlike solid earth, which retains its shape, water changes its form quickly and adapts to its surroundings.[40]

The Role of Water in Life: Life itself depends on water. The human body, animals, and plants require water for survival. Life is a combination of sensations and movements, which are driven by innate heat (Harārat-e-Gharīziyya). This heat enables essential bodily functions required for survival. However, for this heat to be effective, a medium is needed that resists its effect, preventing excessive loss. Water, being cold and moist, serves this purpose by preserving the body's fluids. If the body loses too much moisture, life cannot continue.[3,23,110]

Water is a fluid, meaning it moves and spreads easily. This property allows it to dissolve substances quickly compared to solids. This is why people drink more water than they consume solid food. While water itself does not provide nutrition, it aids in digestion and absorption of food. It also helps maintain the body's moisture levels by replenishing lost fluids.[3,23,110]

Water in Nature: Water exists in all three states of matter: solid (ice), liquid (water), and gas (water vapor). It is found everywhere in nature, from vast oceans to frozen ice caps and even as clouds in the sky. The majority of Earth's water is salty seawater, but it also exists in freshwater sources like rivers, lakes, and underground reservoirs. About 60% of an adult human body consists of fluids, mostly water mixed with ions and other substances. Most of this fluid is inside cells (intracellular fluid), while about one-third is outside cells (extracellular fluid). This extracellular fluid constantly moves throughout the body, ensuring the transport of molecules necessary for sustaining life. Without water, cells cannot function properly.[110]

Water is crucial for maintaining the body's internal balance, known as homeostasis. It helps regulate temperature, supports digestion, and ensures proper nutrient absorption. The shape of cells is influenced by the amount of water inside and around them. Too much water can cause cells to burst, while too little can make them shrink. The body's ability to control water movement ensures stable cellular function.[3,23,110]

Water and Biological Functions: Water plays an essential role in respiration. The blood, which contains water, picks up oxygen from the lungs and transports it to cells. At the same time, it collects carbon dioxide from cells and carries it back to the lungs for removal. Water also aids digestion by dissolving nutrients such as carbohydrates, fats, and proteins. These nutrients are absorbed into the bloodstream and transported to the liver, where they are processed into usable forms. The liver also detoxifies harmful substances, which are then removed from the body with the help of water.[133]

The endocrine system, which produces hormones, also relies on water. Hormones are transported through the bloodstream to different parts of the body to regulate functions like metabolism, growth, and mood.

Unique Physical and Chemical Properties of Water: Water is tasteless, odourless, and a universal solvent, meaning it can dissolve a wide range of substances. This property makes it an excellent medium for transporting nutrients and waste in the body. Additionally, water is a good conductor of electricity, which allows nerve cells to communicate through electrical and chemical signals.[110,133]

Water molecules are made up of two hydrogen atoms and one oxygen atom (H_2O). The hydrogen atoms carry a positive charge, while the oxygen atom has a negative charge. Opposite charges attract, so hydrogen atoms from one water molecule are drawn to the oxygen atoms of another, forming hydrogen bonds. These bonds give water its unique characteristics.[133]

One such property is that ice floats on water. Normally, substances become denser when they freeze, but water behaves differently. As it cools below 4°C, it expands instead of contracting. This means ice is less dense than liquid water, allowing it to float. This is vital for aquatic life. If ice sank, lakes and oceans would freeze from the bottom up, making life impossible in cold climates. Instead, the ice remains on the surface, insulating the water below and allowing life to continue.[133]

Water remains in liquid form over a wide temperature range. This is crucial for life. Imagine if water boiled at 20°C—on a hot day, the water inside living organisms would turn to vapor, causing cells to die. Similarly, if water froze at higher temperatures, life in colder regions would not survive.

Because water remains liquid over a broad range, it ensures the stability of life even in extreme temperatures.[133]

Another important property is water's high specific heat capacity. This means it requires a lot of energy to change its temperature. For example, the specific heat of ammonia is 0.47 J/g°C, while water's is much higher. If Earth's oceans were made of a substance with a lower specific heat, such as ammonia, the temperature would fluctuate drastically. This could lead to severe climate changes, including extreme heatwaves and freezing periods. However, because water absorbs and retains heat efficiently, it helps regulate global temperatures and maintain a stable climate.[133]

Water is truly a miraculous substance essential for the survival of all living things. It not only provides a medium for biological processes but also regulates temperature, supports digestion, and sustains ecosystems. Its unique physical and chemical properties ensure that life can continue even in harsh conditions. Without water, life as we know it would not be possible.[133]

Rukn-e-Hawā (Air)

Anaximenes 611-544 BC Assumed that *Hawā* (air) was the only primary substance and all things came into being from it and they dissolved into it again; just as our souls, being air, held us together, so breath and *Hawā* (air) embrace the whole universe.

The reason about air as the chief component of all things, was based on the assumption that without moistness nothing could have a concrete shape and it was air which possessed moistness in abundance than other *Arkān*. Hence, due to abundance of moistness, air can easily accept different shapes. He also stated that when the temperature of air was intensified, it become fire, and when it was condensed due to decrease in temperature, it become water and on further condensation, it assumed the status of earth. This clearly showed that other *Arkān* were changed forms of air. On the basis of the above-mentioned description, it can be stated that the primary *Rukn* is air, and all things present in cosmos were different forms of the thickness of air.[1,16,]

Air is a simple substance that, due to its lightness, naturally exists between water and fire. It is warm and moist in nature. When air is present in a body, it creates lightness, softness, and porosity. When light elements like air and fire mix with heavier elements like water and earth, different substances form. If water and earth are more dominant, plants come into existence. If earth is dominant along with some qualities of fire and air, animals are formed. The habitat of animals depends on the dominant element in their bodies. For example, birds have more air, which allows them to fly and live in high places like trees. All living organisms survive on three essential components: spirits (Arwāḥ), moisture (Ruṭūbat), and fundamental body parts (A'za Aslia). Since these components constantly decrease over time, they need to be replenished to maintain life.[5,14,40]

Respiration is a vital process that helps keep the body's natural heat (*Hararat-i-Gharīziyya*) at a balanced level. It also nourishes the *Rūḥ Ḥaiwāniya* (vital spirit) and supports the formation of *Rūḥ Nafsāniya* (mental spirit). This balance is maintained by breathing in cool air, which helps control the heat in the heart and removes waste vapours (*Dukhāni Bukhārat*) through exhalation.

For this process to work properly, the air must be moderately cool to prevent excessive heat buildup. The body requires a steady intake of such balanced air because respiration plays a key role in maintaining life. The *Rūḥ* (spirit) is produced from the fine vapours of blood (*Laṭīf Akhlāṭ*), which must also have a balanced temperament. This balance in blood depends on the body's natural heat, which is influenced by consuming the right amount of food, drink, and other substances. Therefore, respiration is essential for sustaining the *Arwāḥ* (spirits) and, ultimately, life itself.[23]

Air is the essential substance that forms the essence of *Rūḥ* (spirit), while water is the essence of *Ruṭūbat* (moisture) and nourishment for the body's organs. Since *Rūḥ* is hot and very light, it dissolves quickly. This is why the body needs air constantly and immediately. Unlike food, which animals can survive without for days, air is necessary every moment—without it, survival is impossible even for a few minutes.

Air is the most common and essential element that influences both animals and humans. It surrounds the body closely and is needed more than anything else. The entire body functions through three vital forces: *Quwwat-e-*

Nafsāniya (mental force), *Quwwat-e-Ḥaiwāniya* (vital force), and *Quwwat-e-Ṭabiyya* (natural force). These forces perform their roles through *Arwāḥ* (spirits), which depend on external air. Because of this, air is the most crucial and ever-present necessity of life. The body is constantly surrounded by air, which easily enters through wide and narrow pores on the skin, reaching every part of the body.[3,22]
Air is a natural substance (*Jism-e-Ṭabai*) that has both active and passive properties, meaning it always affects the body in some way. When air becomes hot, it increases heat in the heart, making the entire body warm. Hot air also draws blood toward the skin, causing redness and leading to the gradual dissipation of the body's natural heat (*Harārat-i-Gharīziyya*). On the other hand, cold air slows down this heat loss at first, but if it gets too cold, it penetrates deep into the body and can completely extinguish *Harārat-i-Gharīziyya.*[3]
Since *Harārat-i-Gharīziyya* is the source of life, its presence is essential for survival. Without it, life cannot continue. For this reason, philosophers have emphasized not just the importance of air but also the need for air with balanced qualities neither too hot nor too cold to sustain and maintain life.[3]

Air is a mixture of different gases in a fixed proportion, consisting of 78% nitrogen, 21% oxygen, 1% carbon dioxide, and small traces of other gases. This specific composition forms *Rukn Hawā'* (Air) and is essential for sustaining life. If this balance is disturbed, the continuation of life may be at risk.

Oxygen is one of the most crucial components of air. During respiration, animals take in oxygen, while plants use carbon dioxide for photosynthesis, and certain bacteria utilize nitrogen. The balance of oxygen in the atmosphere and the amount used in respiration is perfectly regulated. As scientist Michel Denton pointed out, even a slight increase in atmospheric oxygen could be harmful. If oxygen levels were to rise by just 1% above the normal 21%, the global temperature would increase, and the likelihood of forest fires would rise by 70%. This highlights the importance of maintaining the correct oxygen proportion in the air. Similarly, carbon dioxide plays a significant role in trapping heat on Earth, preventing infrared rays from escaping and thus helping to maintain the planet's temperature.[133]

Another key characteristic of air is its density, which is closely related to atmospheric pressure. Air has a unique cohesive force that is stronger than the viscosity of water, making it essential for life. The lungs use energy to facilitate respiration, and air helps make this process efficient. Air naturally resists movement, but the presence of different gases reduces this resistance, making it easier to breathe. If air were more resistant, the lungs would need to work much harder. For example, pulling water into a syringe is easier than pulling honey because honey is thicker and more viscous. If air had a higher resistance, breathing would become as difficult as drawing honey into a syringe.

If air's viscosity, pressure, or fluidity were reduced even slightly, breathing would become much harder. Some might argue that widening the airways could help, similar to using a wider syringe to load honey. However, if the lung's blood vessels were widened, blood would flow too quickly, leaving insufficient time for the exchange of oxygen, carbon dioxide, nutrients, and waste products. This could lead to nutrient deficiencies and waste accumulation in the body. In fact, waste removal is even more critical than nutrition—while a body can survive for some time without food, it cannot function without excreting waste. If blood vessels became too wide, blood pressure would drop, making survival difficult.

Conversely, if the blood vessels were too narrow, their surface area would be reduced, and gas exchange would become inefficient. Oxygen would not reach the body in sufficient amounts, and carbon dioxide removal would also be impaired. The body's ability to absorb oxygen depends on air's current viscosity, fluidity, and pressure, all of which are perfectly suited for respiration.[133]

Air pressure is another vital factor in sustaining life. If air pressure were reduced by one-fifth of its current value, it would lead to excessive evaporation from seas, rivers, and lakes, filling the atmosphere with water vapor and raising global temperatures. On the other hand, if air pressure were doubled, evaporation would slow down significantly, leading to reduced rainfall and widespread drought, turning large areas of the world into deserts. In both cases, life would become unsustainable.[131]

Another important property of air, particularly oxygen, is its ability to dissolve in water. The body absorbs oxygen because it dissolves in blood, where haemoglobin carries it to cells. Cellular enzymes then use oxygen to produce energy. All complex organisms rely on this process for survival. If oxygen's solubility in water were reduced, only a small amount would enter the bloodstream, depriving the body of the necessary energy. However, if oxygen dissolved too easily, its concentration in the blood would become dangerously high, leading to oxygen toxicity and even death.[131]

Thus, *Rukn Hawā'* is the complete composition of air, not just oxygen alone. Some people mistakenly believe that only oxygen represents *Rukn Hawā'*, but this view ignores the true nature and integrity of the concept. The entire balance of gases, pressure, viscosity, and solubility makes air suitable for life. Any disruption to these factors would threaten the survival of living beings.

Rukn-e-Nār **(Fire)**

Heraclitus 540-475 BC believed that fire is the primary element from which everything originates. He saw fire as the source of all matter, with its constant transformations giving rise to all things and eventually dissolving them. For Heraclitus, fire symbolized perpetual change because it transforms substances without being a substance itself. He famously said, "This world, the same for all, was not created by gods or men; it has always existed, still exists, and will always exist as an eternal, ever-living fire." He described fire as continuously flaring up in parts and dying down in others. **Heraclitus** became known as the philosopher of "flux and fire" because of his famous statement, "All things are flowing." He emphasized that transformation is not random but governed by a divine rationality or cosmic principle called *logos*. Fire, as a transforming power, is not destructive but a force of constant renewal.

A key aspect of Heraclitus' philosophy is the **"unity of opposites."** He taught that opposites depend on each other for existence—there is no day without night, no summer without winter, no good without bad. He argued that fire was the central element among water, air, and fire, and that water and air were simply forms of fire.

Heraclitus summarized his philosophy with the idea that **"All things are an exchange for fire."** He believed that the universe is in a permanent state of change, driven by the transformative power of fire.

Fire is a form of heat or energy. Its *Mizāj* is ***Ḥārr and Yābis***. It is required in the compound to make the things light and to provide a stable shape. Its existence within organism brings about ripeness, amelioration, and unity. It occupies a position above the Air. The *Quwat* of fire causes the penetration of air everywhere in all bodies and ameliorates the extremeness of *Water (Mā)* and *Arḍ*. (1,3,16,)

Ibn Harwi classified the *Hotness* into four types

i. Heat of fire

ii. Heat of sun

iii. Heat yields during motion

iv. Heat found in the living organism i.e. innate heat.

In the early atmosphere of Earth, many inorganic molecules were freely available. At that time, the Earth's temperature was extremely high, making it impossible for chemical reactions to occur. Because of this, all inorganic atoms remained in an unstable state. However, as the Earth gradually cooled down, conditions became suitable for chemical interactions. Elements like carbon, hydrogen, nitrogen, sulphur, and phosphorus, along with water vapor, began reacting with each other to form simple molecules such as methane, ammonia, carbon dioxide, and urea. With continued reactions, these simple molecules eventually led to the formation of amino acids, which are the building blocks of life.

This chemical process continued over time. Simple organic and inorganic molecules combined to create more complex organic molecules. Some of these complex molecules reacted with oxygen to form sugars and other essential compounds. The combination of these biomolecules eventually led to the emergence of the first living organisms—simple prokaryotic life forms like bacteria.

These early bacteria developed around hydrothermal vents in the deep ocean, where hot water provided a suitable environment for biochemical reactions. The heat acted like a catalyst, supplying the energy needed for chemical bonds to form. This energy allowed large molecules to be produced, which became the foundation for more advanced forms of

life. Over time, self-replicating macromolecules appeared, leading to the development of more advanced bacteria.
Thus, heat (referred to as *Rukn Nār*) played a crucial role in both the origin and continuation of life. After millions of years, simple prokaryotic cells evolved into more complex eukaryotic cells. The main difference between these two types of cells is that eukaryotic cells have specialized structures such as a nucleus and mitochondria. The nucleus contains genetic material, while mitochondria, often called the "powerhouse of the cell," generate energy for various cellular functions.
Unlike early bacteria, which depended on external heat sources like hydrothermal vents to survive and replicate, eukaryotic cells could produce their own energy through mitochondria. This gave them a significant advantage, allowing them to spread into different environments beyond the ocean vents. As a result, life expanded and evolved into various forms, eventually leading to the diversity of organisms we see today.
For example, modern plants, animals, and humans all have eukaryotic cells with mitochondria. Without this energy-producing structure, life as we know it would not have been able to survive and adapt to different habitats, from deep oceans to forests, deserts, and even extreme cold regions. (9,133,134)
Ibn Rushd stated that the basic arrangement of elements first takes place in plants, and the second level of arrangement occurs in animals. This suggests that plants were the first

living organisms. Plants grow and survive by using earth, water, air, and heat. They absorb water and minerals from the soil, take in gases from the air, and obtain energy from sunlight. Without any of these essential elements—especially heat or air—life cannot continue. Therefore, just like other essential elements, heat (*Rukn Nār*) is necessary for the evolution and survival of life.

All living things go through a cycle of growth, maturity, and ultimately decline, leading to death. To prevent species from disappearing, reproduction is necessary. Plants reproduce through fruits and seeds, and sunlight plays a key role in ripening fruits. Without exposure to sunlight, plants struggle to grow, and even if they do, they remain weak.

The second level of element arrangement occurs in animals. All animals depend on plants either directly (by eating them) or indirectly (by eating plant-eating animals). Animals cannot survive without food. They reproduce through fertilization, which requires sperm and eggs. Semen is produced from blood, and blood is formed from bodily fluids (*Akhlāṭ*, or humors), which come from the digestion of food. For food to be properly digested and transformed, heat is essential. Similarly, plants (which serve as food) need water to grow, and rainwater forms from clouds. Clouds, in turn, are created over oceans and rivers with the help of sunlight (heat). This means that heat plays an essential role in the formation of semen, directly or indirectly.[8,29]

A human body is formed by the combination of male and female reproductive fluids. The male's seminal fluid is considered active, while the female's is passive, and both have moisture. The female's seminal fluid contains more earthly and watery elements, while the male's fluid has fierier (*Nāriyya*) and airy (*Hawāiyya*) elements. When these two fluids combine, they form a zygote, which is naturally moist. Because moisture makes materials easy to shape, the zygote also requires earthy (*Ajzā' Arḍiyya*) and fiery (*Ajzā' Nāriyya*) elements to provide stability and structure. The earthly element gives hardness, while the fiery element provides firmness, making the zygote thick, strong, and stable—though not as hard as stone. This stability prevents the zygote from breaking apart.[14]

According to **Galen (*Jalinoos*),** innate heat is a fundamental force in biological processes. It influences many aspects of life, including gene expression, muscle contraction, enzyme activity, and nerve function. In essence, innate heat is a key factor in maintaining life and bodily functions.[33,39]

Every cell in our body has the same DNA residing within its nucleus. Yet each of this cell type is vastly different. Then why and how the different organs are formed. Obviously, genes do not determine the fate of a cell. Besides, genes some other factors are also responsible for it. Genes are activated and suppressed during the development of a foetus depending on the local environment in which the cell is embedded, resulting in expression of cell that will eventually perform a specific function within a specific organ. This process is highly dynamic and interdependent with a variety of environmental factors playing role in shaping gene expression throughout the organisms.

The external environment is changeable so there is need of constant internal environment of the body for the proper functioning and coordination between the cells and organs. This consistency of internal environment is called homeostasis. Lack of *Hotness* (warm) disrupts homeostasis as dehydration also does.

Different cells require a constant supply of energy to maintain their proper functions and co ordinations. A decrease in the supply of energy whether as free heat or ATP will bring down specialized function of the cell, tissue and body. In severe cases, the damage will be irreversible and ultimately death can occur.

According to law of energy, energy neither created not destroyed only it can change from one form to other form. When we speak of energy as produced it really mean that it was being transformed. Living organisms has a system of energy. It is part of total energy system on earth; hence energy system supports our life. One is within living organisms and other is much larger surrounding us.[133]

Chapter 3

Philosophy of Life and Death

"Life is like riding a bicycle. To keep your balance, you must keep moving." — Albert Einstein

---

Since the beginning of human thought, people have tried to understand the reasons behind life and death. Why and how does birth happen? How do the stages of life unfold? What causes life and death? And why is death unavoidable? Humans have always sought answers to these important questions. Many, throughout history, have wished for long life or even immortality. Like, Gilgamesh, the legendary king of Uruk in Mesopotamian mythology, is famously known for his quest for immortality in the **Epic of Gilgamesh**, one of the oldest literary works in history. After losing his close friend Enkidu, Gilgamesh becomes deeply troubled by the reality of death and seeks a way to escape it. His journey reflects humanity's timeless desire to overcome mortality and achieve eternal life.[111]

In his search, Gilgamesh meets Utnapishtim, a man granted immortality by the gods after surviving a great flood. Utnapishtim shares the secret of immortality with Gilgamesh, involving a plant that restores youth. However, despite finding the plant, Gilgamesh loses it to a serpent, symbolizing the elusive nature of immortality. Ultimately, Gilgamesh learns that true immortality lies in his legacy—his deeds, the city of Uruk, and the lasting impact of his life.[111]

This story highlights the human struggle to accept mortality while emphasizing the importance of living a meaningful life and leaving behind a lasting mark on the world.

In modern times, **Michael Jackson**, the famous pop star, was very interested in staying young and healthy for as long as possible. He took great care of his appearance with skincare routines and surgeries to maintain his iconic look. He reportedly tried unusual ways to live longer, like sleeping in a special oxygen chamber that he believed could slow aging and heal his body. Jackson was also curious about new medical technologies that might help people live longer lives.

His wish to stay young and healthy was not just about living longer—it was also tied to his desire to always look and feel his best. This made his interest in longevity an interesting part of his life story.[136]

Bryan Johnson, a tech entrepreneur and founder of Blueprint, is a pioneer in the field of longevity and health optimization. He invests millions annually in cutting-edge health research and practices to slow aging and enhance longevity. His approach combines advanced technology, rigorous data analysis, and science-backed protocols to monitor and optimize his body. Johnson follows a strict daily routine, including personalized nutrition, exercise, and sleep strategies, designed to maximize his biological potential. He collaborates with leading scientists and experts to measure biomarkers and improve his physical and mental health. Johnson's work inspires a growing movement of people focused on extending health span, not just lifespan. His efforts highlight the potential of science and technology to redefine aging and human health. However, the truth is that death is inevitable. As Jorjani says, death is not something that can be avoided through treatment or remedies.[115]

According to **Ibn Rushd** "Medicine is the practical knowledge of established principles that relate to the preservation of human health and the removal of diseases, and its goal is the human body," the way the philosophy of life and death is explained in Unani Medicine is not found in other sciences. Physicians have specifically divided the field of medicine into two major parts: one is theoretical and the other is practical. The practical part is further divided into two categories:[22,29]

1. Knowledge of maintaining health in healthy bodies, known as ***Ilm-e-Hifz-e-Sehat*** **(Hygiene).**
2. Knowledge of treating diseases in sick bodies, known as ***Ilm-e-Ilaj*** **(Therapeutics).**

The philosophy of life and death is particularly discussed in *Ilm-e-Hifz-e-Sehat* (Hygiene). This section talks about the measures taken to protect health. If a person follows the principles of hygiene, they can naturally live up to 120 years. Ibn Sina (Avicenna) provided an in-depth discussion on the philosophy of aging and death, explaining that the goal of *Hifz-e-Sehat* is not to prevent death or protect against external threats. Instead, it focuses on two main tasks:[22,48]

1. To prevent any damage or corruption to the body's innate moisture *(Rutoobat Ghareeziyah).*
2. To protect the body's innate moisture and heat from premature dissolution and decay.

This shows that *Ilm-e-Hifz-e-Sehat* does not prevent death, as death is inevitable. Physicians divided *Ilm-e-Hifz-e-Sehat* into three categories:

1. **Tadbeer-e-Abdan Za'ifah**: This involves the care of naturally weak bodies, like children, the elderly, and those weakened by bad practices, such as those who fall ill suddenly.
2. **Taqaddum Bil-Hifz:** This focuses on individuals showing signs of weakness or those at risk of illness or changes in health.
3. **Hifz-e-Sehat:** This refers to the care of people who are in perfect health and show no signs of weakness. This is the general and unrestricted approach to health maintenance.

Definition of Life:[38]

1. Life is the preservation of breathing and sensation.
2. Life is the preservation of the body from transformation, changes in qualities, and corruption of the faculties.

3. Life is the continuation of the animal soul, sensory soul, and natural soul in their natural states within the body.

Definition of Death:[38]

1. Death is the transformation of the body towards total corruption.
2. Death is the decay of the organs and the inability of the organs to function due to the failure of the animal soul and other vital powers.
3. Death is the general corruption of the animal body and the withdrawal of bodily powers at the time of corruption.
4. Death is the destruction of the powers present in the animal body.
5. Death is the corruption of the systems that maintain health through their structure and organization.
6. Death is the disruption of the arrangement of elements that maintain the life of the body, which depended on their organized and combined state.

Unani Perspective on Life and Death: Life is a quality that requires sensation and movement. This sensation and movement are made possible through *Innate heat (Hararat Ghareeziyah)* (innate heat). *Innate heat* enables the essential functions for the survival of the animal body, such as absorbing beneficial substances, expelling harmful ones, and processes like digestion and assimilation. These functions cannot occur without *Rutoobat Ghareeziyah* (innate moisture), as it nourishes and protects the *Hararat Ghareeziyah*. The body is a moist and fluid entity, much like oil in a lamp. Just as a fire in one part of a room can warm the entire space, *Innate heat* spreads from the heart to the whole body, keeping it warm. This heat is a common tool for all bodily functions.[22,23]

According to **Galen (Jalinoos)**, *Rutoobat Ghareeziyah* is the fundamental moisture that is an integral part of the body. The presence of *Innate heat* is what prolongs life and age. The span of life depends on the balance of this innate heat. Aristotle says every breathing organism survive on three things, faculty of digestion, *Innate heat and* food. [(14)]

Ibn Abbas Majusi believed that life and its continuation depend on the balance of *Hararat Ghareeziyah*, which is maintained through breathing, balanced nutrition, and proper hydration. Breathing helps maintain the balance of *Innate heat* and nourishes the animal soul, allowing the creation of the psychic soul. The balanced cool air inhaled during breathing cools the excessive heat in the heart, while the vapours from the innate heat (produced by blood) are expelled.[23]

Just as lighting a fire in one part of a room warms the entire space, *Innate heat (Hararat Ghareeziyah)* spreads from the heart to the whole body, keeping it warm. *Innate heat* is directly linked to life, and it is its imbalance or corruption that leads to death. Therefore, the balance of *Innate heat* is essential for maintaining good health. The *Quwat-e-Haywaniyah* (vital power) helps maintain this balance.

The source of *Innate heat* and the vital spirits is the heart. However, the heart's inherent power doesn't always have the capacity to continuously produce *Innate heat (Hararat Ghareeziyah)* and the vital spirits. Therefore, through breathing, the spirit takes in external air, which helps refine and shape the animal power. The innate heat then nourishes this spirit, keeping it alive.[22]

This is why *Quwat-e-Haywaniyah* is superior to other powers in the body, it is essential for the interaction between the spirit and *Harārat Ghareeziyah.* If this balance is disrupted, such as by blockage or excess, it can lead to sudden death.

According to Unani medicine, the initial formation of the body occurs from two substances: the male sperm and the female sperm and menstrual blood. The male sperm is considered active, while the female sperm and menstrual blood serve as the material or substance. The male sperm contains more of the *Hawā'īyah* (air) and *Nāriyah* (fire) components, while the female sperm and menstrual blood contain more of the *Mā'īyah* (water) and *Arḍīyah* (earth) components. Both sperm and menstrual blood have a *warm and moist* temperament, but the heat and moisture in menstrual blood are greater than in sperm.[22,136]

The origin of the embryo starts from a moist substance, with the initial form of the sperm being moist. However, heat overpowers this moisture, causing continuous transformation. Once the male and female substances combine, the heat begins to thicken and solidify the sperm, allowing for the development of various parts of the body under the influence of ***Quwat-e-Musawwirah*** (the formative power).[22,48]

When the baby is born, it cannot sit or stand due to excessive moisture in the body. As the body's *Innate heat (Hararat Ghareeziyah)* works on these excess fluids, the moisture gradually dries up. This drying process allows the child to gain control over movements such as sitting, walking, running, and other activities. Eventually, the moisture diminishes and vanishes, and since *Innate heat* is linked to the moisture, it also diminishes, leading to aging and eventually death.[22,136]

In Unani medicine, three major causes of aging or the increase in age are discussed.

1. Coldness and dryness of temperament: As age increases, the body becomes colder and drier, which affects life, as heat and moisture are essential for sustaining life.
2. Weakness of innate heat (Hararat Ghareeziyah): Over time, the natural heat of the body weakens, contributing to the aging process.
3. Weakness of the faculties (Quwat): As the body's faculties weaken, various organs suffer from a lack of strength, making the body more susceptible to diseases.

In response to these changes, treatments are used to enhance the natural heat and bodily strength.

The male and female sperm (nutfah) from which human life begins, must undergo certain changes for the body to form properly. If the sperm remains overly moist and fluid without drying, the body cannot develop fully or acquire strength and vitality. The drying process is essential for the body to develop its abilities, strength, and motor functions. Therefore, the body must experience a certain level of dryness to achieve full growth and development.[22,136]

This drying process continues gradually as the body matures, leading to the final stage where the body's vital moisture (Rutoobat Gazeeziah) begins to diminish. Since the natural heat (Hararat Ghareeziyah) is linked to this moisture, as the moisture disappears, the heat also diminishes, leading to the eventual cessation of life.[22,135]

Thus, with age, the process of dehydration continues, and eventually, all the bodily moisture is depleted, causing the natural heat to extinguish, leading to death. Understanding this process of dissolution and the need for replenishment is crucial in maintaining health and preventing premature aging.

Explanation of "Badal Ma tahallal" (Replenishment of Degradation):[24,22,136] The human body is constantly undergoing processes of breakdown, decay, and transformation. To maintain balance and prevent the body's temperament from deviating, nature continuously generates actions that replace the material being broken down. For this reason, living organisms need a constant supply of air, water, and food for survival.

As **Ibn Rushd (Averroes)** stated, air, water, and food are essential for living beings because during life, the body's fluids are constantly subject to decomposition and decay. What we can control is our effort to prevent or slow down this decay, thereby extending life. However, the breakdown of bodily fluids is an inevitable process, and eventually, it leads to death. Similarly, the decay of bodily fluids is a frequent occurrence, and its ultimate result is death. Both internal and external factors contribute to the decomposition and decay of bodily fluids:[29]

1. **External factors:** Air, which not only facilitates the breakdown of fluids but can also cause them to become infected.
2. **Internal factors**: The body's innate heat (Hararat Ghareeziyah), which breaks down bodily fluids, and the same heat, which can also cause infection in these fluids. Furthermore, imbalance in the Six Essential Factors (Asbab-e-Sitta Zarooriya) is a major cause of this decay.

Thus, the body continuously replenishes what is being broken down, striving to maintain its balance and prevent premature decay, although complete escape from this process is impossible, and it ultimately leads to death.

From the Perspective of the Elements- When the heavier elements (water and earth) combine with the lighter elements (air and fire), various actions and reactions take place, resulting in the formation of all things in the world. To sustain these things, continuous replenishment of matter

(Badal Ma tahallal) is necessary. Without this replenishment, the body will disintegrate, and life will cease.
As **Razi** (a prominent Islamic physician) said, two factors contribute to the preservation of anybody:[8]

1. No decomposition occurs in the body, like in minerals such as gold and silver.
2. The body receives continuous replenishment of matter to replace what is being lost.

The first task of nature in living beings is to maintain form and balance. For the preservation of form, it is essential that the body's temperament (Mazāj) remains in equilibrium. Since temperament consists of opposing qualities, the actions and reactions of these qualities generate heat, which causes continuous breakdown and decay (Tahallul) in the body. Additionally, the surrounding air and external heat also contribute to this decay.
The decay happens in the constituent elements (Arkan) of the body. Some elements break down quickly, while others take longer. Lighter elements (fire, air) accept decay more easily and rapidly, whereas heavier elements (water, earth) resist decay more slowly.[14,29]
In conclusion, the balance between opposing elements in the body determines its ongoing sustenance and longevity. Without the proper replenishment of matter, the body would fail to maintain its form and function, leading to death.
The decay of the earth element (Rukn Arz) is very slow and minimal. This is why objects that are earth-based or have a dominance of the earth element tend to decompose slowly,

such as minerals and non-living things. Similarly, animals and plants that have a strong presence of the earth element also experience less decay, which contributes to their long lifespans. Examples of such long-living creatures include turtles, elephants, and certain trees like Shisham (North Indian rosewood) and Sagwan (Teak).[14]

Additionally, in many living organisms, extreme weather changes, food shortages, and the need to survive lead nature to initiate certain processes that drastically slow down decay. This allows for longer life. In modern biology, this is similar to the processes of hibernation and estivation, where animals enter a prolonged state of dormancy. During this period, their heart rate, breathing, and metabolism slow down drastically to preserve vital heat and moisture.[40]

Hibernation and aestivation play an important role in helping animals live longer by protecting them from extreme weather and food shortages.

Hibernation is a deep sleep that helps animals survive the cold winter when food is hard to find. Animals like bears, hedgehogs, and bats slow down their heartbeats and breathing, using very little energy. Since they don't move much, their bodies experience less stress and damage, which can help them live longer. Hibernation also protects animals from predators because they stay hidden in safe places like burrows or caves. By conserving energy and reducing physical activity, hibernation slows aging and helps these animals survive harsh winters year after year.

Aestivation is similar to hibernation but happens in hot and dry seasons, especially in deserts. Animals like frogs, snails, and lungfish go into a deep rest when there is little water or food. They burrow underground or hide in moist places to avoid drying out. By staying inactive, their bodies use less energy, preventing dehydration and exhaustion. This helps them survive extreme heat and drought, increasing their chances of living longer.

Both hibernation and aestivation give animals a break from difficult conditions. By avoiding harsh weather, predators, and starvation, their bodies stay healthier for a longer time. The slow metabolism during these resting periods reduces body wear and tear, helping animals extend their lifespan. These survival strategies are nature's way of protecting animals and ensuring they can live through tough times.

Human temperament is closest to balance, with the elements in the human body being relatively equal in proportion. All four elements are more or less capable of undergoing decay, but the lighter elements decay faster. Therefore, nature provides replenishment for these quickly decaying elements accordingly. On the other hand, elements that decompose slowly also receive slower replenishment.

Thus, all living beings unconsciously acquire decayed matter to maintain balance in their temperaments. Just as nature urges living beings to seek food and environments that suit their temperaments, it also guides them to places and situations where the contrast with their temperament is minimal, and where decayed matter is easier to obtain. This helps maintain the body's equilibrium and overall health.[22]

Four Qualities and Life and Death: Many philosophers argue that among the four qualities (Hot, Cold, Wet, and Dry), Heat and Moisture hold fundamental and essential roles, while Cold and Dryness are considered to be non-essential and hypothetical. According to Galen, if a living being has a strong presence of heat and abundant natural moisture, its lifespan will be long and its life will be healthy. According to Greek physicians, Heat and Moisture are the principles of life, while Cold and Dryness lead to death. If either heat or cold dominates the active force in a body, that body will be strong and endure for a longer period. A body with a balanced composition will have a longer life and will remain stable for a prolonged duration.[29]

How does Death Occur?[29]

In Kamil al-Sana'a, **Majusi** writes that, according to Galen, death occurs due to one of the following reasons:

1. **Disruption of the Brain's Composition**: The malfunctioning of the brain results in the failure of the vital force, preventing it from reaching the lungs, thus making respiration impossible and leading to the extinction of vital heat.
2. **Disruption of the Soul's Vital Force**: The malfunctioning of the soul's vital force causes the body to fail in sustaining its natural functions, leading to the extinction of vital heat.

3. **Disruption of Vital Heat:** The deterioration or imbalance of vital heat is the primary cause of death. According to Galen, death is ultimately a result of the disruption and imbalance of this vital heat.

Hence, understanding the factors that disrupt the balance of Innate/vital heat is crucial. The following are the internal causes that influence this:

1. **Organ Malfunctions:**
   - **Brain**: If there is a dysfunction in the brain, the vital force is nullified, preventing the proper transfer of air to the lungs. This results in respiratory failure and, consequently, the extinguishing of vital heat.
   - **Heart**: A malfunction in the heart disables the vital force, preventing it from maintaining necessary bodily functions. This leads to respiratory failure and extinguishing of vital heat.
   - **Liver**: If the liver fails, it loses its ability to generate blood, thus depleting the necessary material for maintaining vital heat, like how a lamp extinguishes when the fuel is gone.
2. **Disruption of Vital Heat's Quality:**
   - **Excessive Heat**: If there is an overabundance of heat, such as from intense fever or a potent warming substance like Corium, vital heat is drained away.

- **Excessive Cold:** If the body experiences intense cold, such as from cold medications (e.g., Opium or Hemlock), vital heat is suppressed and the bodily fluids freeze, similar to how a lamp goes out in a cold room.

3. **Disruption of Body's Material Composition**:
   - **Deficiency of Body Fluids**: Excessive hunger, thirst, or significant blood loss depletes the body's fluids, which causes vital heat to diminish, just like a lamp going out when it runs out of oil.
   - **Overaccumulation of Humors**: When the body accumulates excess fluids, such as alcohol or overfeeding, it results in congestion, preventing air from circulating properly, leading to a decrease in vital heat and potential death.

In essence, death is primarily caused by the imbalance or failure of vital heat, either through internal organ dysfunction, extreme conditions of heat or cold, or deficiencies or excesses in the body's material composition.

External Causes of Disruption of Vital Heat: After discussing the internal causes, we now look at the external causes that can disrupt or diminish vital heat. These external factors lead to the cooling or extinguishing of the body's inherent warmth, eventually causing the cessation of life. The following are the different external causes:

1. **Sudden External Release of Vital Heat:** When vital heat suddenly escapes and disperses, it leads to the cooling of both the external and internal parts of the body. This situation often occurs in cases of extreme emotional states, such as during an intense emotional outburst (e.g., "Shadi Marg," meaning sudden death due to intense joy). This is similar to how a flame is extinguished when a strong wind blows across it, causing it to cool down.
2. **Sudden Internal Accumulation of Vital Heat**: This occurs in conditions like extreme fear or acute illnesses, which cause the internal vital heat to concentrate and remain trapped within the body. This leads to coldness in the extremities (e.g., cold hands and feet), as the external body cools down while the internal heat accumulates and is unable to dissipate.
3. **Drowning**: When the body is submerged in water, the capacity for breathing is lost. This leads to internal congestion and the reduction of vital heat, similar to how a lamp's flame goes out when the wick is submerged in oil, reducing its ability to burn.
4. **Suffocation (Choking):** When there is a lack of breathing (such as in cases of choking), toxic or waste gases accumulate in the heart, disrupting vital heat and causing it to extinguish. This is similar to

how a flame is extinguished when it is covered, preventing the air from feeding it.

5. **Exposure to Foul, Decaying Vapours**: If vital heat comes into contact with foul, decaying, or putrid gases, such as when cleaning dirty sewers or areas with toxic vapours, it causes disruption. The nature of vital heat in such a case resembles that of a flame that is extinguished when exposed to smoke or noxious fumes.
6. **Venomous Bite or Poisonous Exposure**: The heat from the venom or the extreme temperature of the poison (either hot or cold) can disturb the body's internal vital heat. The disruption caused by poison is similar to the destruction of a flame due to the intrusion of an external force that alters the flame's quality.

In summary, the external causes that affect vital heat include sudden release or accumulation of heat, drowning, suffocation, exposure to harmful gases or toxins, and venomous bites. Each of these external disruptions causes the body's internal warmth to be depleted or altered, ultimately leading to death.

What is Natural Death: Natural death is a process that results from the gradual depletion of vital moisture (Ruṭūbat g̱harīzīyah) in the body, which protects and sustains the body's innate heat (Harārat g̱harīzīyah). During the early stages of life, particularly in youth, the amount of vital moisture is greater than the heat, which helps the body thrive and grow. As a person progresses through adulthood, the balance starts to shift, and vital moisture begins to decrease, eventually becoming less than the heat it was once meant to protect.[22]

In the later stages of life, particularly in old age, the body's vital moisture continues to diminish, and the protective role it once had over vital heat weakens. As the moisture diminishes, it is unable to be replaced fully by nutrition or other means. Over time, this ongoing depletion leaves the body without the necessary moisture to sustain its vital heat, causing the body's internal processes to gradually fail. This leads to the eventual loss of vitality and, ultimately, death.

The process of natural death varies from person to person, depending on their individual temperament and how their vital moisture is consumed or depleted throughout life. For some, this process might take longer, while for others, it may occur more swiftly. Differences in lifestyle, environment, health, and even emotional factors can also influence how and when vital moisture is used up, thus affecting the timing of death. Ultimately, the natural death process is driven by this gradual breakdown of the balance between vital moisture and heat, a process that is irreversible and unique to each individual.[22]

Factors that reduce innate heat (*Harārat g̲h̲arīzīyah*) in the body include emotional stress like anger, fear, and excessive joy; physical strain such as overexertion or lack of rest; imbalanced diet, including extreme hunger, thirst, or overeating; exposure to harsh environmental conditions like cold, heat, or pollution; excessive sexual activity, poor sleep patterns, and overexercising. Chronic illnesses, harmful foods, and external stressors like disturbing sights or sounds can also weaken innate heat. These factors, when frequent or excessive, can deplete the body's energy, leading to health issues and a shorter lifespan.[14,22,24,29,40]

According to **Ibn Sina**, the following factors can increase heat and warmth in the body:[1,22,48]

1. Eating moderate amounts of food.
2. Engaging in activities that involve heat, like working in hot environments or exposure to warm air, hot oils, or heating pads.
3. Moderate physical activity and exercise.
4. Mild massage and skin treatments.
5. Avoiding excessive bleeding or treatments that cause loss of blood like cupping, as this leads to cooling instead of heating.
6. Using warm foods and medicines.
7. Taking moderate baths in warm water.
8. Engaging in moderate mental activities like thinking, without excess.
9. Experiencing mild anger or frustration, which generates heat.
10. Experiencing moderate happiness, which increases warmth.
11. Having the skin's pores contract, which traps heat and increases body temperature.

The philosophy of medicine revolves around understanding the six essential factors which are: air, food and drink, physical movement and rest, mental activity and calm, sleep and wakefulness, and retention and evacuation. These factors are essential for life and health; their balance maintains health, while imbalance leads to disease. If one adheres to these principles, they can live a long and healthy life, as seen in historical examples where longevity was common. In modern times, people in places like Japan, Switzerland, and Singapore enjoy longer lifespans due to their adherence to these principles and the favourable geographical influences.

In modern medicine, various theories on aging and death are presented, such as:[54]

1. Cross-linking/Glycation hypothesis of aging
2. Evolutionary senescence theory
3. Theory of antagonistic pleiotropy (Disposable soma theory)
4. Genome maintenance hypothesis
5. Neuroendocrine hypothesis
6. Oxidative damage/free radical hypothesis
7. Rate of living theory
8. Replicative senescence hypothesis.

These theories provide insights into the complex processes behind aging and the maintenance of health throughout life.

In Unani medicine, the philosophy of life and death is explained in terms of innate heat and innate moisture along with the factors that affect them. This theory is clear and scientific, and cannot be overlooked at any level.

Chapter 4

Biodiversity in Unani Perspective

"Nature's variety is its greatest strength." — Charles Darwin

---

- **Tibb-e-Unani as the name suggests, originated in Greece or Unan. It was the Greek philosopher-physician Hippocrates (460-377BC) who freed medicine from the realm of superstition and magic and gave it the status of science. Tibb Unani (Unani system of Medicine) is the knowledge of various state of human body with respect to health and disease. It offers a complete way of healthy living for preservation and promotion of health and its restoration if lost. The theoretical frame work of Tib is based on the teachings of Hippocrates. He recommended that whenever and where ever possible drugs should be gentle and safe. This is the main objective of Tib. After Hippocrates, a number of Greek scholars enriched the system and it imbibed the best from the medicine that was being practiced in Egypt, Syria, Iraq, Persia, India, China and other Middle east and far East countries. That's why the system**

is known in different parts of the world by different names, like Greco-Arab medicine, Ionian medicine, Arab or Islamic medicine, Oriental medicine and so on. [1][2]

The fundamental principle of the Unani system recognizes that disease is a natural process and symptoms of a disease are body's reaction to disease. The chief function of the physician is to aid the natural forces of the body specially Tabiyat-e-badan.

"**Tabiyat** - Kamale Awwal means the most suitable movement of any compound." [2]

The Tib is based on the Humoral theory-which presupposes the presence of four humours. They are Dum (blood), Balgham (phlegm), Safra (yellow bile) and Sauda (black bile). The body has the power of self-preservation to maintain a correct balance of these humours, which is called as Quwwat-e-Mudabbira (Medicatrix natura). Unani medicines help the body to regain this balance. [1][2][3]

The essential constituents and the working principles of the body, can be classified into seven main groups: Arkan or primary building blockers, comprising Earth, water, Air and Fire the building blocks of all three creatures (Mawalide salasa) in the universe. Mizaj (Temperament); Akhlat (humours); Aaza (organs); Arwah (life, spirits or vital breaths); Quva (capacities) and Afaal (functions). Each of the four elements has its own special qualities: **Earth** is cold and dry; **Water** is cold and moist; **Fire** is hot and dry; **Air** is hot and moist. The temperament of a substance may be a

Mizaj-e-moatadil (balanced one) or a Mizaj-e-ghair-moatadil (imbalanced one). [4][5][6][7][8]

Different types of imbalanced temperaments are described in Tib. At birth every person is endowed with a unique and healthy humoural constitution which determine the temperament of the individual.

Tib also postulates that the body contains a self-preservative power, which strives to restore any disturbance within the limits determined by the constitution or state of the individual the power known as Tabiyat or Quwwate mudabbire badan. The physician merely aims to help and develop rather than supersede or impede the action of Tabiate Badan. [2]

Under Umoor-e- Tabiya (basic principles), the core ideas and theories of Unani medicine are covered. Classical writings describe these fundamental ideas in logical and philosophical terms. During the time when these ideas and theories were put forward in particular contexts, logic and philosophy were the only available ways of knowing. These theories and notions are difficult to learn and comprehend because of their logical and philosophical framework. Therefore, it is necessary to explain these ideas in the context of today. [9]

Al Umoor al Tabiya elaborates on the principles of Unani medicine and the human body. The ancient scholars tackled every problem of the day and found solutions in the vernacular of the day. The beginning of life continues to be a hotly debated subject.

This biodiversity is the result of three and a half billion years of evolution. Among the various theories of evolution, the theories of Lamarck and Darwin hold significant importance. Lamarck was a biologist and naturalist who observed that animals adapt to their environment and befit themselves for this purpose. For instance, the long neck of the giraffe is due to its ancestors stretching their necks to reach food from tall trees.

Lamarck proposed that changes occurring as a result of the struggle for survival were passed on to the next generation, which continued the evolutionary process. However, Lamarck's theory did not gain acceptance in the scientific community. Two years after Lamarck's death, a young Charles Darwin embarked on a sea voyage on his ship HMS Beagle. Before his journey, Darwin had studied under contemporaries of Lamarck and was familiar with Lamarck's theories of inheritance. During his voyage, Darwin made observations that appeared different from Lamarck's ideas. Based on these observations, Darwin presented his own theory of evolution. [9][10][11]

Lamarck had a great impact on Charles Darwin, who began his scientific career studying geology before developing an interest in biology while on his well-known Galapagos Islands trip. His meticulous studies of the wildlife on the island prompted Darwin to conjecture about the impact of geographic isolation on the emergence of species, ultimately resulting in the development of his theory of evolution.

In 1859, **Darwin** presented his theory in his seminal essay On the Origin of Species. Twelve years later, he finished it with The Descent of Man, which expanded on the idea of one species evolving into another to include humans.

Darwin founded his hypothesis on the concepts of natural selection and chance variation, which would eventually be referred to as random mutation. [10][12]

At the Centre of Darwinian thought stands the insight that all living organisms are related by common ancestry. All forms of life have emerged from that ancestry by a continuous process of variations throughout billions of years of geological history. In this evolutionary process many more variations are produced than can possibly survive, and thus many individuals are weeded out by natural selection, as some variants outgrow and out-reproduce others. [10][11]

These basic ideas are well-documented today, supported by vast amounts of evidence from biology, biochemistry, and the fossil record, and all concern scientists are in complete agreement with them. The differences between the classical theory of evolution and the emerging new theory center around the question of the dynamics of evolution -the mechanisms through which evolutionary changes take place.[9]

Darwin's own concept of chance variations was based on an assumption that was common to nineteenth-century views of heredity. It was assumed that the biological characteristics of an individual represented a 'blend' of those of its parents, with both parents contributing more or less equal parts to the mixture. This meant that an offspring of a parent with a useful chance variation would inherit only fifty percent of the new characteristic, and would be able to pass on only twenty-five percent of it to the next generation. Thus, the new characteristic would be diluted rapidly, with very little chance of establishing itself through natural selection. Darwin himself recognized that this was a serious flaw in his theory for which he had no remedy. (10)(11)

Darwin recognized the significance of pre-existing variation within any population of organisms. In nature, there is an ongoing struggle for survival, and those animals better adapted to their environment are more likely to survive. Darwin termed this process "natural selection." Successful organisms pass on their traits to the next generation, leading to gradual changes in a species over time. These changes occur very slowly and progressively. After nearly twenty years of diligent work, Darwin published his research. Alfred Russel Wallace, who independently conceived a similar theory of natural selection, also contributed to the understanding of evolutionary processes. (10)(11)(12)

Abu al-Hasan Nizam al-Din Ahmad bin Umar bin Ali Samarkandi, known as "**Nizami Aruzi**," was one of the distinguished scholars of the sixth century Hijri. In his work **"Chahar Maqala"** (Four Discourses), he discusses a theory resembling evolution. Nizami Aruzi posits that among inanimate objects, **clay** is the primary element and **coral** the final product, with coral serving as a bridge between the mineral and plant kingdoms (coral is a stony organism that grows like a tree under the sea, particularly in the waters of Yemen and Andalusia, and is harvested by divers). In the plant kingdom, he identifies **thorns** as the first and **date palms and grapes** as the final stages. The **grapevine** acts as an intermediary between the plant and animal kingdoms, seeking refuge from the parasitic vine that strangles the trees it entwines. [13]

In the animal kingdom, the first creature is the **worm**, and the final one is the **ape** (or wild man), found in the forests of Turkistan. This ape, known as "**Banmanus**" is seen as a link between humans and animals. Reading Nizami Aruzi's account, one might speculate that this early concept of evolution foreshadowed what later became known as Darwin's theory. [13]

According to the Unani System of Medicine, it is clear that the concept of arkan had been proposed to address the origin of life. In this concept four arkan were considered to be the elementary building blockers of animals, plants and minerals, and also the way these four arkan raise so many diverse species of Muwaleede salasa. Obviously, the next step that needs to be addressed was of biodiversity. The concept of temperament was put forward to explain the diversity amongst creatures. Present day sciences attribute the biodiversity to the genetic and environmental variations besides the ecosystem. The Darwin's theory of survival of the fittest explains the origin of new species purely on the basis of interaction of the attributes of biodiversity. [9]

An Overview of Biodiversity

In essence, every element of the universe is worthy of contemplation and reflection, which is why humanity has always been curious about the creation of the universe and its fundamental components. Human perception and sensations are quite limited, while human creativity and formation are both challenging and complex. The knowledge bestowed by nature has always been the focus of human study, leading to the development of various sciences associated with human existence. Some sciences have remained at the conceptual level, such as theology, while others, directly related to the human body, are known as the medical sciences. (15)

Efforts have continuously been made to understand all sciences related to the human body, initially from a conceptual perspective and subsequently from a research and analytical viewpoint. In this way, various sciences have been employed to fully comprehend the human body in order to uncover the mysteries of how human existence came to be and why maintaining human health has always been a fundamental aspect from the very beginning. (16)

After the continuous discovery of sciences, the study of genes presents in the human structure in thc current era is particularly noteworthy. This is because genes are like a book that contains all the information about human existence. Therefore, today's scientists strive to unlock this book of genes and obtain all the information unique to each individual, allowing for the analysis of every aspect of human health and disease. In ancient times, thinkers also endeavored to understand human creation progressively and comprehend the order of formation. Many philosophers developed their own theories on this subject, among whom Aristotle is particularly notable. [16]

In Unani medicine, various theories have been proposed to understand all these discussions, such as Empedocles' theory of Element, the theory of Temperament, Buqrat's theory of Akhlāṭ (Humors), and the theory of the Kayfiyāt Arbaʻa. All these theories are deeply interconnected, and studying them separately without considering their interrelations makes it difficult to grasp the art comprehensively. The theory of Element Arbaʻa is also referred to as "**Ummahat**" because the term "Um" (mother) signifies the origin of a child's birth, as the child comes into existence from the mother. Similarly, the ʻAnāṣir serve as the foundation and origin for all existing things. [2][3][14]

By understanding the proportion of these ʻAnāṣir, we can comprehend the proportion of their Kayfiyāt, which in turn causes differentiation and formation in all existing things. Therefore, the most fundamental and important theory is that of the Kayfiyāt Arbaʻa, which encompasses the entire field of medicine. Physicians attribute the differences and diversity in the Mawālīd Thalātha (animals, plants, and minerals) to the differences in Temperament and consider the variation in Temperament responsible for this diversity. [9][14][17]

Modern experts have presented the theory of biological diversity to explain these differences and diversity. They attribute this to environmental and genetic variations. According to this theory, environmental and genetic traits are responsible for the diversity and differences found in living beings. Environmental diversity has the potential to bring about functional and structural changes in living beings. Similarly, genetic differences among various living beings are also responsible for functional and structural diversity. There are also some other factors mentioned that contribute to this diversity. [(18)(19)]

Historical background:

After 3.5 billion years of evolution, the biodiversity exists today. The term "Biological Diversity" is shortened to "Biodiversity." Since Norse and McManus (1980) defined it for the first time, the latter usage seems to have gained popularity about that time. It appears that Walter G. Rosen coined the term "biodiversity" in 1985 during the inaugural planning meeting of the "National Forum on Biodiversity," which was held in September 1986 in Washington, DC (UNEP 1995). The idea of biodiversity and the term "biodiversity" were popularized among scientists and the general public to describe diversity at all levels of biological organization, from populations to biomes, by the published proceedings of this meeting, which were published in a book titled Biodiversity (Wilson and Peters 1988). The United Nations Conference on Environment and Development

(UNCED) held in 1992 at Rio de Janeiro (Rio Summit or Earth Summit) has also substantially elevated the status of Biodiversity. [(18)(19)(20)]

Definition of biodiversity: Bio denotes life, while diversity is uniqueness or variety. Therefore, the diversity of life forms on Earth and the fundamental interdependence of all living things are referred to as biodiversity. As a broad phrase for organisms present in the living world, biodiversity refers to the quantity, variety, and variability of living things. As a result, it may be taken to mean "Life on Earth," "diversity of life and its processes", "condition of being different" or even "Life's unending forms," as described by Darwin in 1859. When considered broadly, biodiversity really is "the essence of life" (Frankel, 1970). But in actuality, biodiversity is a very broad and intricate notion with implications that permeate every aspect of human existence and endeavour. A vast range of living things, including plants, animals, and other microscopic organisms, that coexist in a habitat are referred to as biodiversity, also known as biological diversity. In addition to human activity, topography and climate have a significant impact. [(18)(19)(20)]

Biodiversity is the variability among living things from all sources, including terrestrial, marine, and other aquatic ecosystems and the ecological complexes of which they are a part. This definition was given during the UN Earth Summit in 1992. This covers diversity among species as well as diversity across species and regional ecosystems. It is the primary functional element of a natural ecosystem and represents the diversity of organisms and their relative frequencies within an ecological system.

In our biosphere immense diversity exists at all levels of biological organisation ranging from macromolecules within cells to biomes. sociobiologist Edward Wilson describe the combined diversity at all the levels of biological organisation. The most important of them are– Genetic diversity, Species diversity and Community/Ecosystem diversity. [18][19][20]

1.**Genetic diversity**: Genetic diversity includes variations in the quantity and types of genes that make up a species' genetic makeup as well as genetic variation within a single species. It also includes genetic variance across different populations within the same species. Numerous molecular methods can be used to quantify genetic diversity. India boasts over 50,000 distinct genetic variations in paddy and over 1000 variations in mango. A species' gene variation rises with habitat and size diversity. As a result, several races, variations, and subspecies are formed. Due to genetic variability, Rauwolfia vomitoria, a medicinal plant found in many Himalayan regions, exhibits variations in the concentration and effectiveness of its active component, reserpine. The development of adaptations to shifting environmental situations is aided by genetic variety. [18][19][20]

2.**Species diversity:** Species diversity refers to the variety in number and richness of the species in any habitat. The number of species per unit area at a specific time is called species richness, which denotes the measure of species diversity. The Western Ghats have greater amphibian species diversity than the Eastern Ghats. The more the number of species in an area the more is the species richness. The three indices of diversity are - Alpha, Beta and Gamma diversity. (11)(18)(19)(20)

i. **Alpha diversity**: It is measured by counting the number of taxa (usually species) within a particular area, community or ecosystem.

ii. **Beta diversity**: It is species diversity between two adjacent ecosystems and is obtaining by comparing the number of species unique to each of the ecosystem.

iii. **Gamma diversity:** It refers to the diversity of the habitats over the total landscape or geographical area.

3.**Ecosystem diversity:** Ecosystem diversity is the variety of habitats, biotic communities, and ecological processes in the biosphere. It is the diversity at ecosystem level due to diversity of niches, trophic levels and ecological processes like nutrient cycles, food webs, energy flow and several biotic interactions. India with its alpine meadows, rain forests, mangroves, coral reefs, grass lands and deserts has one of the greatest ecosystem diversities on earth. (10)(11)(18)(19)(20)

Magnitude of Biodiversity: The globe is a lovely place to live because of the vast array of living things that we share this planet with, including plants, animals, and microorganisms. There are living things practically everywhere, from the tops of mountains to the bottom of the ocean, from deserts to rainforests. Scientists estimate that there are between 70 and 100 lakh species on Earth. Their size, shape, color, and attitude are all different. The earth's extraordinary diversity of life constitutes an integral and important component of it, but the growing human population is posing major dangers to biodiversity. Climate, terrain, and human activity all have a significant impact on biodiversity, also known as biological diversity. (18)(19)(20)

Every species, regardless of size, contributes significantly to the ecosystem in biodiversity. In addition to preserving the natural equilibrium, it promotes societal advantages across a region, including tourism, education, and research. It supports the upkeep of ecological processes, soil formation, nutrient recycling, climate regulation, waste degradation, and disease prevention. It offers an ecosystem's health index. All living forms (plants and animals) in the biosphere must exist and be in good health for the human race to survive. (18)(19)(20)

The number of species in a region at any particular time is a common way to quantify biodiversity. The latest estimate of the number of distinct species on Earth is between 8 and 9 million. However, we do not know the actual size of our natural wealth. This is known as the 'Taxonomic obstacle'. So far, around 1.5 million species of microbes, animals, and plants have been identified. Every year, approximately 10-15 thousand new species are identified and published around the world, with invertebrates accounting for 75%. The number of undescribed species is certainly substantially more. India has a high biological diversity due to its unique biogeographical location, diverse climatic conditions, and enormous eco-diversity and geo-diversity. [19][20]

India is classified as belonging to three biomes (Tropical Humid Forests, Tropical Dry/Deciduous Forests, and Warm Deserts/Semi Deserts) and two of the major realms (The Palearctic and Indo-Malayan) in the global biogeographic classification. India is believed to contain more than 8% of all animal species worldwide, although making up only 2.4% of the planet's land area. This percentage accounts for roughly 92,000 species that are known. In terms of area, India is the seventh-largest nation on Earth. With its diverse habitats, including hills, valleys, plateaus, seashores, mangroves, estuaries, glaciers, grasslands, and river basins, India is home to a wide range of ecosystems and biomes. It also shows diverse climates, precipitation, temperature distribution, river flow, and soil. India is one of the 17 major biodiversity countries in the world, with ten biogeographic zones. has distinctive environment and biota. [19][20]

Patterns of Biodiversity Distribution: The distribution of plants and animals is not uniform around the world. Organisms require different sets of conditions for their optimum metabolism and growth. Within this optimal range (habitat) a large number and type of organisms are likely to occur, grow and multiply. The habitat conditions are determined by their latitudes and altitudes, temperature, precipitation, distance from the equator (latitudinal gradient), altitude from sea level (altitudinal gradient) are some of the factors that determine biodiversity distribution patterns. The most important pattern of biodiversity is latitudinal gradient in diversity. This means that there is an increasing diversity from the poles to equator. Diversity increases as one moves towards the temperate zones and reaches the maximum at the tropics. Thus, tropics harbor more biodiversity than temperate or polar regions, especially between the latitudes of 23.5°N and 23.5°S (Tropic of Cancer to the Tropic of Capricorn). [18][19][20][21]

Harsh conditions exist in temperate areas during the cold seasons while very harsh conditions prevail for most of the year in polar regions. Columbia located near the equator has nearly 1400 species of birds while New York at 41°N has 105 species, and Greenland at 71°N has 56 species. India, with much of its land area in the tropical latitudes, is home for more than 1200 species of birds. Thus, it is evident that the latitude increases the species diversity. Decrease in species diversity occurs as one ascends a high mountain due to drop in temperature (temperature decreases 6.5°C per Km above mean sea level). [18][19][20]

The Tropics, located between the Tropic of Cancer and the Tropic of Capricorn, are home to a vast variety of living organisms because they provide the perfect conditions for life to thrive. The climate in these regions is warm and stable, creating an ideal habitat for different species to evolve and grow. Unlike extreme environments like deserts or polar regions, the tropics offer a comfortable temperature range of 25°C to 35°C, which is perfect for most biological and metabolic activities. This allows animals and plants to function efficiently without the stress of extreme heat or cold.

Another important factor contributing to the high biodiversity in the tropics is the abundance of rainfall, often exceeding 200 mm per year. This constant supply of water supports the growth of lush forests, rivers, and wetlands, which in turn provide shelter and food for many species. For example, the Amazon rainforest, one of the most biodiverse places on Earth, is home to millions of plant and animal species due to its warm temperatures and heavy rainfall.

Additionally, the environmental conditions in the tropics remain relatively stable throughout the year. Unlike temperate regions, which experience drastic seasonal changes, the tropics have consistent climate patterns, humidity, and sunlight (photoperiods). This stability allows plants and animals to reproduce and grow continuously without long periods of dormancy or migration.

Moreover, tropical regions have rich soil and plenty of nutrients, supporting a wide range of plant life. These plants, in turn, provide food and shelter for herbivores, which support carnivores, creating a thriving and complex ecosystem. For example, in tropical rainforests, tall trees like mahogany and fig provide food for insects, birds, and monkeys, while large predators like jaguars rely on these smaller animals for survival.

Overall, the combination of warm temperatures, high rainfall, stable seasons, and abundant resources makes the tropics a perfect place for life to flourish. This is why tropical regions contain more species of plants, animals, and microorganisms compared to any other part of the world.

Chapter 5

Philosophy of Equitable Temperament

"The balance of nature lies in the harmony of opposites." — Hippocrates

---

- **In the Unani system of medicine, diversity is explained through the concept of Temperament (*Mizāj*). Every species has its own unique Temperament that is best suited to its survival and well-being. This ideal or balanced Temperament is called *Mu'tadil* (equitable). The main idea is that each species thrives when its Temperament matches its natural environment. This concept is known as the *Philosophy of Equitable Temperament.***

According to **Ali Ibne-Abbas Majusi**, "All types of bodies, whether heavy or light, that exist in this constantly changing world are created by combination of four building blockers (ustuqussat) in varying or consistent amounts based on the body's requirements." This combination causes one or more attributes to take precedence over the body; this is known as Temperament. The word "Imtizaj" in Arabic means "meeting to mix with each other."[3][22][23][24]

The Unani scholars dared to define Imtizaj and its varieties, as well as the combination of ingredients. Two categories are described for it. Two methods of admixing are Imtizaj-e-Sazaj (simple) and Imtizaj-e-Ḥaqīqī(real). Since the sciences developed from philosophy and metaphysics, the way that ancient professionals described merely physical problems undoubtedly had both a philosophical and a metaphysical undertone. Therefore, it is important to consider the definition and description of imtizaj and, by extension, Temperament from a proper perspective, particularly in light of the early stages of evolution. First, all the definitions apply to inanimate objects and the simplest type of combination.

All of these alterations may have occurred on the planet before life began, but they may have persisted and helped to create the conditions for life's evolution. As a result, simple and actual mixing may have occurred frequently in the most basic forms of life, such as viruses. (22)(23)(24)(25)

Temperament's classification can be linked to temperament, which comes in two Flavors:

1- Equitable temperament, or Temperament-e-Mu'tadil; comes in two varieties.

(a) Tibbi (Existing) and (b) Ḥaqīqī (Ideal).

2- Mizāj Ghayr Mu 'tadil (Differing Temperament):

Mizāj Mu'tadil Ḥaqīqī (ideal equable temperament) does not exist. As a result, the Unani System of Medicine could never make reference to this hypothetical and supposed temperament. (22)(23)(24)

Mizāj Mu'tadil Tibbi (Existing Temperament) is present in compounds where the constituent parts are not precisely equal in quantity and quality, but they are perfectly balanced in accordance with the characteristics and functions that the compound requires in order for the compound to be useful for its intended purpose. Eight types of Mizāj Mu'tadil Tibbi are further categorized as follows:[(22)(23)(24)]

1-Mizāj Mu'tadil Naw'ī bi'l Qiyās ila'l Khārij (Equable Temerament of a species as a whole):

In the Unani system of medicine and philosophy, every species has its own unique temperament (*Mizāj*), which distinguishes it from other species. This temperament is what allows a species to grow, survive, and reproduce in its natural habitat. As long as the environment remains suitable, the species can thrive without difficulty. However, even small changes in the environment can have a significant impact on survival, and major changes such as shifting to a completely different habitat can be life-threatening.

Take the example **aquatic species** like fish. Fish have a temperament that is adapted to living in water, and their bodies are designed for this environment. However, not all water bodies are the same. A fish from the ocean has a temperament suited for salty seawater, while a freshwater fish is adapted to lakes and rivers. If a saltwater fish is placed in a freshwater pond, it cannot survive because its temperament demands a specific balance of salt and minerals. Even though the medium (water) is the same, the small change in salinity is enough to disrupt its survival.

Similarly, **terrestrial animals** have temperaments suited for life on land. For example, **Siberian** cranes are birds that migrate during winter to warmer regions. Their temperament is not suited for extreme cold, so they move to locations with a climate that matches their needs. This shows that even within the same type of habitat (land), animals need specific environmental conditions to survive.

The Role of Temperamental Range in Survival

While species have a general temperament that defines them, there is always some variation within that range. The wider the range of temperament a species has, the more adaptable it becomes. Species with a very narrow temperament range can only survive in specific conditions, whereas species with a broader range can live in multiple environments.

For instance:

- **Polar bears** have a cold and dry temperament, making them well-suited for freezing Arctic conditions. However, they would struggle to survive in a hot desert because their bodies are not adapted to high temperatures.
- **Camels**, on the other hand, have a warm and dry temperament, which makes them perfect for desert life. They store water in their bodies and tolerate extreme heat, but they would not survive in the Arctic due to their inability to handle extreme cold.

Humans: The Most Adaptable Species: Among all species, humans (*insān*) are the most adaptable because they have the broadest range of temperament. Unlike animals, humans can survive in extremely cold places like Siberia as well as in hot, humid regions like the Amazon rainforest.

This is because humans have a natural ability to adjust to different climates through clothing, shelter, food, and technology. For example,

In cold regions, people wear thick clothing, build insulated homes, and eat warm, high-energy foods to maintain their body heat.

In hot deserts, people wear loose, light-coloured clothing, build houses with ventilation, and consume cooling foods to stay hydrated and cool.

This ability to adapt to different environments is why humans are considered the most flexible and resilient species. In Unani philosophy, human temperament is referred to as **"Temperament-e-Ashraf"** or **"the best of all temperaments"**, because it allows people to live in diverse environments and adjust to changes better than any other species.

So, every species has a temperament that defines its ideal living conditions, and even small environmental changes can impact its survival. Some species, like fish and birds, have very specific temperamental needs, while others, like camels and polar bears, have adapted to extreme conditions. However, humans have the greatest flexibility in temperament, allowing them to thrive in nearly every environment on Earth.

This adaptability is what makes human temperament superior and the most balanced among all living beings.[22][23][24][25][26]

2- Mizāj Mu'tadil Naw'ī bi'l Qiyās ila'l Dākhil (Most Equable Temperament of a member of the species):

Every species has a general temperament (*Mizāj*) that defines its overall characteristics. However, within the same species, each individual has its own unique temperament that makes it different from others. This individual temperament is called *Mizāj Mu'tadil Naw'ī bi'l Qiyās ila'l Dākhil* (Most Equable Temperament of a Member of the Species).

While the species as a whole may have a certain temperament suited to its survival, an individual's temperament may slightly differ based on its body composition, lifestyle, and environment. For example, humans as a species have a general temperament, but each person has their own specific balance of hot, cold, moist, or dry qualities. What is suitable for one person may not be ideal for another. Some people can tolerate heat better, while others are more comfortable in cooler climates.

A person's temperament usually falls within a natural range that is common for their species. However, humans and other living beings have a certain flexibility in their temperament, allowing them to survive in different environments and at different stages of life. For example, a child generally has a warmer and moister temperament, while an elderly person tends to have a colder and drier temperament. Similarly, a person may adapt to a colder climate over time, even if they were originally from a warmer region.

This natural adaptability helps individuals adjust to different conditions, ensuring survival and a balanced state of health throughout life.[22][23][24][25]

3- Mizāj Mu'tadil Ṣinfī bi'l Qiyās ila'l Khārij (Equable temperament of a race):

In the Unani system of medicine, temperament (*Mizāj*) is not only unique to individuals but also applies to different races. Each race has its own specific temperament that makes it distinct from others. This racial temperament is best suited to the natural environment and lifestyle of that particular group.

For example, people living in colder regions, such as those from Arctic areas, tend to have a naturally warmer (*Har*) temperament, which helps them withstand extreme cold. On the other hand, people from hot desert regions, like the Sahara, often have a cooler (*Barid*) temperament to help them endure high temperatures. These differences in temperament are inherited and have evolved over generations to ensure survival in specific climates.

Although there is some flexibility in temperament within a species, the range for racial temperament is more limited. This means that while a human being can adapt to different environments to some extent, a person from a tropical region may still struggle to adjust fully to life in the Arctic and vice versa. Their bodies are naturally designed for the climate and conditions where their ancestors lived.

This racial temperament is important because it helps maintain the distinct characteristics of different groups over time. It influences physical traits, endurance, and even certain behavioural tendencies that are beneficial for survival in their specific environment. For instance, people from high-altitude regions like the Himalayas have developed a temperament and physical traits that allow them to live in low-oxygen conditions, while those from coastal regions are more adapted to humid and salty environments.

In short, racial temperament plays a key role in preserving the unique identity and survival advantages of each race, ensuring that they are best suited to their natural surroundings. [22][23][24][25]

4- Mizāj Mu'tadil Ṣinfī bi'l Qiyās ila'l Dākhil (Most Equable Temperament of a member of the race):

In the Unani system of medicine, temperament (*Mizāj*) is not only specific to species and races but also varies among individuals within the same race. Even though a race has a general temperament that sets it apart from others, each person within that race has their own unique temperament, which may differ from their fellow members. This individual temperament within a race is called *Mizāj Mu'tadil Sinfi bi'l Qiyās ila'l Dākhil* (Most Equable Temperament of a Member of the Race).

For example, people from a tropical region may generally have a cooler temperament (*Barid*) to help them withstand the hot climate. However, within that race, some individuals may have a slightly warmer or drier temperament than others, affecting their ability to handle heat differently. Some may sweat more, while others may feel less discomfort in high temperatures. These small variations exist even though the overall racial temperament remains the same.

It is relatively easy to determine the collective temperament of a species or a race by observing common traits shared by most members. For instance, polar bears as a species have a warm (*Har*) temperament suited for freezing Arctic conditions, while camels have a dry temperament adapted to desert life. Similarly, people from colder regions generally have a warmer temperament compared to those from hotter climates.

However, identifying the one individual within a species or race who has the *most balanced* and *most moderate* temperament is extremely difficult. This is because determining such a person would require analysing the temperament of every individual within that race or species at a given time, which is nearly impossible. There may be someone who has the perfect balance of all temperamental qualities, but since temperaments vary slightly from person to person and change over time due to age, diet, and environment, identifying that exact person is highly challenging.

In short, while species and racial temperaments can be identified in general, pinpointing a single person with the most perfectly balanced temperament within a race or species is nearly impossible because of the natural variations among individuals.[22][23][24][25]

5- Mizāj Mu'tadil Shakhṣī bi'l Qiyās ila'l Khārij (Equable Temperament of an Individual as a whole): In the Unani system of medicine, every individual has a unique temperament (*Mizāj*) that is best suited for their body and daily functioning. This individual temperament is different from the overall temperament of their race or species. While a race has a general temperament that most of its members share, an individual's temperament is more specific and has a narrower range. What is ideal for one person may not be suitable for another, even within the same race or family.

For example, two people from the same region may have different temperaments—one may have a warmer (*Har*) temperament, while the other may have a cooler (*Barid*) temperament. This affects how they respond to the environment, food, and lifestyle. A person with a warm temperament may prefer cooler climates and lighter foods, while someone with a cold temperament may feel comfortable in warm weather and prefer hot meals.

Even though an individual's temperament has some flexibility, it plays a key role in their overall well-being. It helps maintain their health, supports their ability to reproduce, and ensures their survival. The adaptability of this temperament allows people to adjust to different phases of life, such as childhood, adulthood, and old age. It also helps them cope with changes in their health, work environment, and weather conditions. For instance, as people age, their temperament may shift slightly, requiring them to change their diet and lifestyle accordingly. A young person with an active metabolism may tolerate heavy, oily foods, but as they grow older, they might need lighter meals to maintain good health.

Since a person's temperament is unique, no two individuals, whether from the same race, country, or even family are exactly alike. This is why the Unani system of medicine treats each person as an individual rather than as part of a group. Unlike modern medicine, which often focuses on diagnosing and curing a disease, Unani medicine takes a holistic approach. This means that instead of just treating an illness, the Unani doctor considers the patient's overall temperament, lifestyle, and environment to restore balance in the body.

This ancient approach aligns with what modern medicine now calls "**holistic treatment,**" a concept that has become popular today. In Unani medicine, the goal is not just to cure a disease but to maintain overall health and well-being. That is why a person must consider their temperament when making choices about their daily life—such as diet, job, clothing, and living conditions. For example, someone with a dry (*Yabis*) temperament should avoid too much spicy or fried food, as it can increase dryness in the body, leading to imbalances. Similarly, a person with a cold temperament should dress warmly in winter to maintain their internal balance.

Unani Philosophy emphasizes that understanding one's temperament is essential for maintaining good health and making the right lifestyle choices. This personalized approach ensures that treatment and daily habits are tailored to each individual, promoting overall well-being.[22][23][24][25]

6- Mizāj Mu'tadil Shakhṣī bi'l Qiyās ila'l Dākhil (Equable Temperament of an Individual during youth):

A person's temperament (*Mizāj*) is not fixed throughout life. It changes as they grow older and go through different stages of life. To maintain good health at each stage, temporary or permanent adjustments in temperament are necessary. Childhood, adulthood, and old age each have different temperamental needs, and the body naturally adapts to these changes.

For example, children generally have a warmer and moister temperament (*Har wa Ratb*), which supports their rapid growth and high energy levels. This is why they need more nutritious, easily digestible food to support their development. On the other hand, elderly people tend to have a colder and drier temperament (*Barid wa Yabis*), which makes them more prone to joint pain, weakness, and slow digestion. To maintain balance, they may need warmer foods, herbal tonics, and a more relaxed lifestyle.

Illness can also cause temporary changes in a person's temperament. For instance, if someone with a normally balanced temperament falls sick with a fever, their body may become temporarily hotter and drier than usual. A skilled Unani doctor will analyse these changes and use natural remedies, diet adjustments, and lifestyle modifications to help restore the patient's normal temperament and overall health.

The temperament that is considered ideal for a person change depending on their age and condition. However, the most balanced and natural temperament occurs during youth, when the body is at its peak strength and functioning. This temperament during a person's prime years is called *Mizāj Mu'tadil Shakhsi bi'l Qiyās ila'l Dākhil* (Most Equable Temperament of an Individual). It is not necessarily the best temperament for all stages of life, but it is the most suitable for that particular time.

For example, a young adult in their 20s or 30s generally has a strong metabolism, high energy levels, and good immunity. Their body can tolerate a variety of foods and physical activities. However, as they move into middle age or old age, their temperament naturally shifts, and they may need to be more mindful of their diet, exercise, and lifestyle choices to stay healthy.

In conclusion, a person's temperament is dynamic and adapts to their age, health, and environment. Understanding these changes helps in maintaining a balanced and healthy life. Unani medicine recognizes this and focuses on adjusting a person's lifestyle and treatment according to their temperament at different stages of life.(22)(23)(24)(25)

7- Mizāj Mu'tadil 'Uḍwī bi'l Qiyās ila'l - Khārij (Equable Temperament of an Organ): Different organs within the same body have different structures and functions. Because of this, each organ requires a specific temperament (*Mizāj*) that is best suited to its role. This means that no two organs have exactly the same temperament, even though they all work together to keep the body functioning properly. The temperament that is most suitable for a particular organ is called *Mizāj Mu'tadil Uzwi bi'l Qiyās ila'l Kharij* (Most Equable Temperament of an Organ).

For example, the heart is responsible for pumping blood throughout the body. To perform this function, it needs to be warm and slightly dry, as warmth keeps the blood circulating, and dryness helps maintain its strength and structure. If the heart becomes too cold or too moist, it may lead to problems like weak circulation or fluid buildup.

On the other hand, the brain, which controls thinking, memory, and nervous system functions, requires a cooler and moister temperament. This helps maintain clarity of thought and proper nerve function. If the brain becomes too hot, it can lead to excessive mental activity, stress, or headaches, while too much dryness may cause forgetfulness or difficulty concentrating.

Similarly, the liver, which is responsible for digestion and metabolism, needs a warm and moist temperament to break down food and produce essential nutrients. If it becomes too dry, digestion may slow down, leading to constipation or nutritional deficiencies.

Each organ has its own unique temperament, which allows it to function optimally. If an organ's temperament becomes unbalanced due to illness, poor diet, or environmental factors, it can lead to health problems. In Unani medicine, treatments aim to restore the natural temperament of each organ so that the body remains healthy and functions smoothly.

In conclusion, just as every individual has their own temperament, each organ within the body also has a specific temperament that suits its role. Recognizing and maintaining the correct temperament of organs is essential for overall health and well-being. [22][23][24][25]

8- Mizāj Mu'tadil 'Uḍwī bi'l Qiyās ila'l Dākhil.(Equitable temperament of an organ in a physiological-functional state): In the Unani system of medicine, every organ in the body has its own natural temperament (*Mizāj*), which allows it to function properly. While this temperament has some flexibility, it is the most specific and limited when compared to the temperaments of individuals, races, and species. This means that an organ's temperament does not change as much as a person's overall temperament, but it can still adapt slightly to different conditions.

An organ goes through three main stages during its lifetime:

1. **Proliferation (Growth Stage)** – This is when the organ is still developing and growing, such as in childhood or early life. At this stage, the organ needs a warmer and moister temperament to support rapid cell growth and development.
2. **Differentiation (Maturity Stage)** – This is when the organ has fully developed and is functioning at its best. At this stage, the organ has reached its ideal temperament, which allows it to perform its functions efficiently.

3. **Decline (Aging Stage)** – As the organ ages, it gradually weakens, and its temperament changes. It may become drier or colder, leading to reduced efficiency and potential health issues.

When an organ reaches full development and is functioning properly within its natural limits, its temperament is called *Mizāj Mu'tadil 'Uḍwī bi'l Qiyās ila'l Dākhil* (Most Equable Temperament of an Organ Internally). This means that as long as the organ is performing its functions normally, its temperament is in balance and remains within the physiological boundaries of health.

For example, the stomach needs a warm and moist temperament to properly digest food. When a person is young and healthy, their stomach maintains this balance, allowing for efficient digestion. However, as they age, their stomach may become drier or weaker, leading to digestive issues such as indigestion or constipation.

Similarly, the lungs require a slightly warm and moist temperament to function well. If the lungs become too dry, it may lead to breathing difficulties, whereas excessive moisture could cause conditions like congestion or phlegm buildup.

Maintaining the correct temperament of each organ is essential for good health. If an organ's temperament becomes unbalanced, it can lead to disease or dysfunction. The goal of Unani medicine is to restore and maintain the natural temperament of each organ so that the body remains in a state of harmony and balance.

In summary, every organ has a specific temperament that is necessary for its function. This temperament changes slightly during different life stages but remains within a narrow range. When an organ is fully developed and working perfectly, it is considered to have *Mizāj Mu'tadil 'Uḍwī bi'l Qiyās ila'l Dākhil*, meaning it has reached its most balanced and optimal state. [22][23][24][25]

Unani philosophers believe that for a species to survive and reproduce effectively, its temperament (Mizāj) should match the qualities of the surrounding environment in degree. This means that living beings should have characteristics that balance the climate they live in. However, if some individuals develop traits that are too different from the ideal temperament, nature ensures they do not become extreme by introducing opposing qualities of the same degree.

For example, people living in Africa, where the climate is extremely hot, should ideally have a cold (Barid) temperament to help them withstand the heat. If they had a hot (Har) temperament, the intense heat would become unbearable, leading to health issues and lower survival rates. On the other hand, those living in the Arctic, where the weather is freezing, should have a hot (Har) temperament. This helps them cope with the cold and function efficiently in their environment.

This principle suggests that opposite traits are essential for survival in extreme climates. Over long periods, individuals with temperaments best suited to their environment thrive and pass on their traits to the next generation. Meanwhile, those whose traits do not align with the environmental demands struggle to survive and eventually disappear.

The ideal and most balanced temperament is called *Mizāj Mu'tadil*, which means "moderate temperament." This is the most suitable state for both the body's structure and its functions, as it develops through continuous interaction with the environment. Once the body is formed with a certain temperament, this balance influences how it functions in daily life

Chapter 6

Relationship in Structure & Function

"The universe is structured so that every function finds its place." — *Ibn Sina (Avicenna)*

- **The way something is built (its structure) determines how it works (function). This idea is important in biology, chemistry, physics, and engineering. In living things, the shape and design of body parts help them perform specific tasks. For example, lungs have tiny air sacs that increase surface area, helping in oxygen exchange. Birds have hollow bones, making them lightweight for flying. Teeth come in different shapes—incisors for cutting, molars for grinding, and canines for tearing.**

In **chemistry**, molecules work based on their structure. Water (H_2O) has a bent shape, making it polar, which helps it dissolve many substances. Carbon dioxide (CO_2) is linear and nonpolar, so it does not mix well with water. The way atoms are arranged also changes how substances react. Cis-fats are liquid and healthy, but trans-fats are solid and unhealthy. The wrong structure of a drug can even cause serious health problems, like in the thalidomide disaster.

In **physics**, the structure of objects affects their movement and stability. Bridges are built in different ways—arch bridges distribute weight well, while suspension bridges use cables for support. In cars and planes, streamlined shapes reduce air resistance, making them faster and more efficient. White clothes reflect heat, keeping us cool, while black clothes absorb heat, making us warmer.

In **engineering** and design, structure helps things work properly. Skyscrapers have flexible steel frames to resist wind and earthquakes. Musical instruments are designed to produce sound efficiently—for example, a violin's curved body amplifies sound, while a flute's tube shape changes pitch. Good design helps machines, buildings, and everyday objects work better.

Even at the smallest and largest scales, structure affects function. Black holes are so dense that they trap light. GPS satellites must adjust for time differences in space due to Earth's gravity. Superconductors let electricity flow without resistance, and quantum dots change colour based on their tiny size. In every field, from nature to technology, understanding structure helps us improve function.

Animal Structure and its Relation to the Environment as discussed in Aristotle's book *Generation of Animals*: Aristotle emphasizes that animal generation is an intricate process with various stages. The development of an animal's structure is shaped by different "causes"—material, formal, efficient, and final causes—which contribute to how an animal takes form and relates to its environment.

In the process of reproduction, Aristotle identifies the male's role as providing the "movement" or heat necessary for fertilization, while the female supplies the material (like menstrual fluid) necessary for the embryo's formation. The balance of "cold" is critical for proper development, and this relates directly to environmental conditions.

Aristotle explains that the environment, particularly temperature, plays a significant role in animal development. For example, certain animals (like marine creatures) thrive in warmer waters, which provide the heat necessary for their generation. The fluidity of water allows marine creatures to take on a wider variety of shapes.

Blooded animals are typically larger and more complex, with their structure forming from a "soul" that provides the essence of life. On the other hand, **bloodless animals** like insects and have different reproductive mechanisms, including spontaneous generation or laying eggs that transform into larvae. Their growth is also influenced by their environment, such as the availability of nutrients.

Animals adapt to their environment through their physical and biological structures. For instance, aquatic animals have specialized adaptations to their habitat, like the formation of gills for breathing in water, or special reproductive strategies to thrive in their specific ecological niches.

Aristotle concludes that all the animal's growth are directed toward a specific end or "purpose," which he describes as the perfection of the individual creature within its natural environment. This teleological view implies that the animal's structure is not random but developed to fu of its life in its environment.

Aristotle's book *Generation of Animals* should give a foundational understanding of how Aristotle connects the structure of animals to their natural environments and how various factors, including temperature, nourishment, and biological roles, influence development.

Empedocles' Theory of Element Arba: According to this theory, everything between the earth and the sky is composed solely of the four 'Anāṣir (earth, water, air, and fire). These 'Anāṣir make up all things, whether living or non-living, humans or animals, plants or minerals. These 'Anāṣir combine to form all compounds and eventually dissolve back into these 'Anāṣir. This understanding indicates that the four 'Anāṣir are eternal, while compounds are perishable. [7][8][16]

Characteristics of the 'Anāṣir: Each of these 'Anāṣir possesses three characteristics: [29][30]

1. **Mādda (Matter):** They have their own Mādda (Matter).
2. **Kayfiyāt (Specific Quality):** They have a unique Kayfiyāt.
3. **Ṣūrat Naw'iyya (Specific Form):** They have a particular Surat (form), known as the Ṣūrat Naw'iyya (Specific Form).

Interaction and Combination of 'Anāṣir: There is a debate among scholars on how these 'Anāṣir combine to form compounds:[30]

1. **Physicians View:** The inherent Kayfiyāt (quality) of the 'Anāṣir is Fa'il, while the intensity of the Kayfiyāt (quality) is Munfa'il.
2. **Philosophers View:** The Ṣūrat Naw'iyya of the 'Unṣur is Fa'il, and its Mādda (Matter) is Munfa'il.
3. *Scholars View:* The Kayfiyāt of the 'Unṣur is Fa'il, and its Mādda (Matter)is Munfa'il.

Since nature does nothing in vain, every Murakkab (compound) is created for a purpose. This purpose gives the compound its Surat, which enables it to perform its specific Fael(function) for which it was created. [30][31]

Ibn Rushd, a notable physician, states that according to natural science, everybody is composed of Mādda (Matter) and Surat. The existence of Mādda (Matter) is for the Surat, and together they create a natural shape that performs specific functions. Aristotle said, "Nature does nothing in vain." This can be understood with examples from human creations. For instance, the combination of wood and the Surat (form) of a boat result in a boat, which then performs its function of sailing on water. [29][32]

When the primary 'Anāṣir combine and interact, a specific Kayfiyāt (quality) arises in the compound, known as Temperament. Different scholars have defined Temperament in various ways:[30]

- **Ali ibn al-Abbas al-Majusi**: Temperament is the predominant Kayfiyāt or Kaifiyaat in a compound.
- **Ibn Sina (Avicenna):** Temperament is the balanced state where no single Kayfiyāt dominates over the others.

- **Ibn Rushd**: Temperament is the condition in which a compound performs its natural Fael (function) or acts Munfa'il, created by the different proportions of the Anāṣir. After acquiring Temperament, a Murakkab (compound) gains a specific Surat (form). Since the Surat (form) depends on Temperament, the Ṣūrat Naw'iyya of the body is the basis of its unique Quwwat, upon which all the compound's Afaal (functions) depend, such as Taghdhiya (nutrition), Tawlīd (reproduction), and Namu(growth). Hence, according to Ibn Sina, the Af'āl (functions) of any compound depend on its Ṣūrat Naw'iyya , and the variation in Surat leads to differences in nature, functions, and properties of bodies. (30)(31)

In Greek medical philosophy, **Af'āl** (functions) and **Quwā** (faculties) are deeply connected and essential for the formation and functioning of the body's organs. The source of the body's various functions lies within the body itself, and this source is called **Quwā**. The body and **Quwā** are not separate; rather, **Quwā** is the *formal cause* (Sabab Suri), while **Af'āl** is the *final cause* (Sabab Tamami) of the body. To fully understand **Af'āl**, one must first understand **Quwā**, as they are closely related. **Quwā** cannot be seen directly but are recognized through the functions (**Af'āl**) they produce. This is why Unani physicians discuss them together.

Each **Quwā** is responsible for specific functions, and every function arises from a particular **Quwā**. They complement each other, working in harmony. Additionally, every **Quwwat** (faculty) needs a balanced level of **Ḥarārat**

Gharīzīyya (innate heat). This heat, provided by **Ṭabī'at** (the body's natural force), ensures that each organ gets the warmth it needs to perform its functions effectively.

The connection between the structure of a cell and its function can be understood through physiology. Different types of cells in the human body have unique shapes and structures, and these differences determine the specific jobs they perform.

For example:

- **Columnar epithelial cells** (found lining the uterus) are long and elongated. Their shape is suited for their job, which is secretion.
- **Cuboidal epithelial cells** (found on the surface of the ovary, in the lining of the nephron, and the walls of renal tubules) have a cube-like shape. This structure helps them perform their functions of absorption and secretion.
- **Ciliated columnar epithelial cells** (found in the respiratory tract and fallopian tubes) have tiny hair-like structures called cilia. These cilia help these cells remove waste or unwanted particles from the body by pushing them out.

Similarly, **phagocyte cells** (a type of immune cell) have extensions called pseudopods. These pseudopods allow them to "engulf" or swallow bacteria and harmful particles, helping to protect the body.

In all these examples, the structure of each cell is perfectly designed for the specific function it performs. This shows how closely structure and function are related in the human body.

In the Unani system of medicine, the functions of the body reflect the faculties, temperament (**Mizāj**), and structure (**Tarkīb**) of the organs. Normal functioning indicates a healthy state, while any disruption in temperament or structure can lead to dysfunction. Unani physicians identify three types of functional abnormalities: **Nuqsan-i-Af'āl** (partial loss of function) happens when coldness (**Burūdat**) reduces activity, such as weak digestion caused by a cold stomach. **Taghyyur Af'āl** (altered function) occurs when excess heat (**Ḥarārat**) or cold disrupts normal processes, like undigested food in the stomach. **Butlān-i-Af'āl** (complete loss of function) happens when extreme cold or heat leads to total dysfunction, such as the stomach completely failing to digest food.

In chemistry, thousands of Murakkab (compounds) known as hydrocarbons are made from just two 'Anāṣir (elements), hydrogen and carbon, combining in different ratios and proportions. These are categorized into groups like alkanes, alkenes, and alkynes, forming numerous Murakkabat (compounds) like methane and ethane. Another example is chalk and marble, both composed of calcium carbonate, yet differing greatly in hardness due to their structure. [21][32][33]

The concept of isotopes in chemistry explains how different arrangements of the same element can produce substances with varied properties. For example, diamond and graphite are both made of carbon but differ drastically in hardness due to the different arrangements of carbon atoms. [30][33]

In the human body, various structures of cells correspond to their different Afʿāl (functions), demonstrating the relationship between **Ṣūrat** (form) and **Fael** (function). Thus, the variation in specific forms, influenced by Temperament, leads to differences in nature, functions, and properties of bodies. From a medical perspective, there is a correlation between Temperament, structure, and Af ʻāl (functions). Afʿāl (Functions) emanate from the Surat (form), and the Surat is dependent on Temperament. Therefore, it can be said that Afʿāl (functions) are also dependent on Temperament. Tabiyat works first to maintain Surat (shape) and Mizāj of any body and for maintenance of shape it is necessary that temperament should remain normal. [24][31][30]

This compatibility is illustrated by the example of a boat: the combination of wood and the Surat of a boat results in a boat that performs its Fael (function) of sailing on water. If the Temperament changes, the compound will disintegrate, and the functions will cease to exist. As mentioned in Aqsarai "The structure of any compound depends on Temperament, and due to this, a change in Temperament leads to the loss of structural and functional relationship."[5]

Chapter 7

Causes of Existence (Asbabe wajood)

"I was a hidden treasure, and I loved to be known. Hence, I created the world." —
Hadith Qudsi

- **Everything in this universe has a cause, which both precedes and binds it, and every set of causes is preceded by another set of causes. Consequently, no entity or group of things may deduct from a universal cause. This relationship between cause and effect is implied to be necessary by their coherence. Because no effect arises on its own, the cause is the condition of the effect.** [(15)(27)]

Aristotle provided numerous biological illustrations of causation, such as the development of sharp teeth for cutting objects into pieces and the flat, practical molars for grinding food. The four fundamental reasons of each of the three creatures Jamādāt, Nabātät, and Haywänät were also elucidated by him. They are Asbāb Ṣūriyya (Formal causes), Asbāb Tamāmiyya (Final reasons), Asbāb Māddiyya (Material causes), and Asbāb Fā'iliyya (Effective causes). [(16)(28)]

These causes are explained by an example of manufacturing of chair as given by Aristotle. Wood is Sabab Māddi or material cause for making chair because wood is a material itself. The special shape and structure of the chair is Sabab Ṣūri or formal cause. Carpenter is the necessary part for the manufacturing because without him matter and shape will not come together, so the carpenter is Sabab Fā'iliy or efficient cause and at last the Sabab Tamāmi or final cause is the purpose of the chair and the reason, for which it is manufactured. [22][24]

With the rise of philosophy in ancient Greece, people began to focus on explaining things in a natural and logical way. One of the first questions Greek philosophers tried to answer was: What is everything in the world made of? To explain this, they came up with the idea of "Elements." However, they could not agree on how many Elements existed. Some believed that everything was made from just one basic substance, while others thought there were two or three fundamental Elements.

Empedocles proposed theory of four *Element*. According to this theory everything in this world i.e. *Mawālīd Thalātha* are made up of four *Element* viz. *Rūkn Arḍ, Rūkn Mā', Rūkn Nār,* and *Air element (Rūkn Hawā')* [3]. This theory became popular among philosophers and later on it was also accepted by *Unani* physicians. Human body is also made up of these four *Element*. Every *Rūkn* serves different purpose in formation of human body. The purpose of *Rūkn Arḍ* and *Rūkn Mā'* is to provide material for formation of body. *Rūkn*

Mā' also serves purpose of adhesion in this material. *Rūkn Nār* provides stability to the shape of the body. The purpose of Air element (Rūkn Hawā') is to make bodies light and porous.

Anaximenes viewed air as a holding substance of universe. He said that "as our soul, being air, holds us together, so do breathe and air surround the whole universe". What he meant by this is that our soul keeps us alive and it is made up of air. Till we are alive our body keeps itself together, but after death soul leaves our body and slowly our body disintegration. Similarly, air which surrounds universe holds it together and prevents it from disintegrating. Anaximenes also said that the earth is flat and floats on air (28).

Anaximenes considered air as God because air provides life. Also, he viewed air as an element that is immeasurable, which precedes all things, and it is also the originator of all things. All these are property of God (33).

Aristotle stated, "The beginning of thought is the end of action, and the end of action is the beginning of thought." The concepts that first come to mind are those that are executed in the last. Similarly, when we delve into the study of Tib, the initial thoughts are about the human body, then the preservation of its health, and finally, how and from what health is achieved. The human body is composed of the 'Anāṣir Arba. The Temperament is created from the combination of these 'Anāṣir, and anybody comes into existence through Madda, Surat, and Kayfiyāt. Therefore, we need to re-analyses the human body to understand various terms related to it, such as Mādda (Matter), Hayūlā (Amorphous substance), Surat, Kayfiyāt, Tabiyat, Istiṭāla, Jauhar, Nafs, Kaun wa Fasad etc., and recognize the relationships between them because it is possible to deduce particulars from universals. [(14)(24)]

Relationship between Hayūlā (Amorphous substance), Mādda (Matter) and Surat:

The philosophical explanation found in Unani Medicine shows that Hayūlā (Amorphous substance), Surat-e-Jismiya, and Ṣūrat Naw'iyya are the main sources that describe the makeup of all existences. The Arabic term "Hayūlā (Amorphous substance)" signifies "primordial matter." The Arabic word for primal substance is known by several names, such as Hayūlā (Amorphous substance), 'Unṣur , Ustuqqus, and Madda. Hayūlā (Amorphous substance) is synonymous with Materia et Forma (Matter and Form) in Latin and Greek. According to Al-Tabari, Hayūlā (Amorphous substance) is the fundamental stuff or essence of a body that is shared by all elements, accepts all divisions, and maintains its integrity through numerous transformations. For instance, while bread, cake, and biscuits all have distinct appearances, they all contain the same kind of protein. As a result, Hayūlā (Amorphous substance), the dove, is evenly dispersed throughout the show. [(14)(34)]

The concept of "Hayūlā (Amorphous substance)" is that, it is inherently existent and capable of receiving various Kamiyat, Kayfiyāt and Surat. Hayūlā (Amorphous substance) has the capacity for quantity and quality, and it is referred to as Raas-ul-Ajsām (substance of all bodies). When Hayūlā (Amorphous substance) acquires a Surat, it is called Madda. Mādda (Matter) is an eternal entity and a Jauhar. Any object that occupies space and has mass is considered Mādda (Matter). Each Mādda (Matter) has its own Surat, and Mādda (Matter) without Surat is called Hayūlā (Amorphous substance). The state of Mādda (Matter) is described by its properties such as weight, volume, quantity, pressure, and temperature. The indivisible particle of Mādda (Matter) is called an "atom," and a combination of atoms forms a "molecule."(14)(32)(35)(36)

Matter exists in three physicals states: solid, liquid, and gas. (32)

1. **Solid**: A state of Mādda (Matter) that does not require a container to assume a shape, has a specific shape and volume, and its constituent parts are stable. Examples include bricks, wood, iron, and ice.
2. **Liquid**: A state of matter that requires a container to assume a shape, does not have a specific shape but has a specific volume, and its constituent parts are stable but can move around. Examples include water, oil, and syrup.
3. **Gas**: A state of matter that instantly fills any container, does not have a specific shape or volume, and its constituent parts move freely and rapidly. Examples include oxygen, carbon dioxide and other gases.

The Arabic word Ṣūrat Naw‘iyya means "form," and Nou' means "species." According to the traditional Unani philosophy, Ṣūrat Naw'iyya is the unique form that sets each being apart from the rest. Every human has a unique personality, structure, function, action, affect, attitude, aptitude, and a host of unique qualities, despite their many similarities. Ṣūrat Naw'iyya is the cause of these characteristics. [(14)(37)(38)]

Surat-e-Jismiya: "Jism is physic, and Surat is form," so the physical form, or Surat-e-Jismiya, of any entity is its physical structure. This Jism may be Murakkab (Compound) or Mufrad or *Basit*(single). A drop of water, for instance, is the same as a million litres of water. It's Baseet Jism, this water. However, the human body is a Murakkab structure made up of several *Ajsām Basita*, such as water, namkiyat (minerals), shahem (fats), and lahem (protein). The Baseet Jism can be further divided into many tiny bits and particles, according to ancient Unani philosophers. This separation may even be made theoretically, if not actually, by Quwwat-e-Wahema (the ability of comprehension). [(14)(37)(38)]

Surat is an eternal substance that shapes the material substance in a specific manner. Surat is neither shape nor Mādda (matter), but Mādda is an eternal thing and Jauhar, while Surat serves as an attribute of the Jauhar. Surat can change from one state to another, but the physical quality of Hayūlā (Amorphous substance) does not change. Mādda (Matter) remains in its state, and its physical form changes, such as giving different shapes to silver objects while the substance of silver remains the same. "Shapes change, names change, but the reality does not."[(5)(14)(37)(38)]

An entity exists inherently due to its Surat. Similarly, an entity exists accidentally due to its **Hayūlā** (Amorphous substance). For Surat to exist, Hayūlā (Amorphous substance) must be present, but Hayūlā (Amorphous substance) does not require Surat for its existence. Hayūlā (Amorphous substance) is a substance that does not change and remains in its state. For example, the door, chair, bed, and cupboard have different Surat(forms), but their Hayūlā (Amorphous substance) (i.e., wood) is the same. Similarly, all animals have different Surat and names, but their Hayūlā (Amorphous substance) is the same: flesh, skin, bones, and muscle. This commonality exists in all. [5][14][37][38]

According to modern scientific understanding, the idea of Nou' (Species) designates the eighth major taxonomic level in the biological hierarchy, which is as follows: Life, Domain, Kingdome, Phylum Class-Order, Family, Genus, Species. There are one or more species in a genus.

According to the above-mentioned remark, the old Ṣūrat Naw'iyya description is nothing more than a modern understanding of species or special forms of 'Anāṣir (elements) in physics and chemistry. As a result, each 'Unṣur (Element) consists of two forms: Physical and Special. 'Unṣur (Element) has three physical forms: liquid, solid, and gaseous, whereas Special form is determined by the structure of its smallest unit.[32][37]

A Jauhar is the smallest unit of any 'Unṣur (Element). As a result, the structure of this Jauhar may be that unique 'Unṣur (Element) shape that is theorized and known in Unani

Classics as Ṣūrat Naw'iyya. The development of numerous scientific tools in the later age allowed for the study of this fundamental characteristic and character, which led to the discovery that Jauhar is the smallest unit of matter known to us as an atom, or Jauhar, and that its structure is known as an atomic structure, or, Ṣūrat Naw'iyya. According to the above depiction, Ṣūrat Naw'iyya is a unique form of each Jauhar (Atom), which together make up the 'Unṣur (Element) and subsequently all Beings. [(5)(14)(37)(38)]

The specific Surat is the characteristic that causes the appearance of an entity. According to Greek philosophy, physical objects in the natural world are composed of two things: Hayūlā (Amorphous substance) and Surat. This concept is called hylomorphism. The specific Surat refers to the particular reality of an entity, from which all its characteristics arise. [(30)]

There are two types of **Surat Jismiya** (physical forms): 1) Kamiyat (Quantity) and 2) Kayfiyāt (Quality). Kamiyat (Quantity) precedes Kayfiyāt (Quality). The existence of Kayfiyāt is associated with Kamiyat. If there is no Kamiyat, there will be no Kayfiyāt either. Kayfiyāt refers to the measure of length, width, and depth of something. [(14)]

Kayfiyāt is a specific attribute whose parts remain intact and together, and which inherently does not accept division nor seeks proportion. Examples include Hotness, Coldness, Moistness (Ruṭūbat), Dryness (Yubūsat), colour, smell, taste, etc. In this context, Kayfiyāt refers to the Kayfiyāt Mizaji obtained from the combination of the four 'Anāṣir, which makes a compound ready to adopt a Ṣūrat Naw'iyya (specific form). Since structure is dependent on Temperament, the different Surat of Murakkab (compounds) are due to their different Temperament. [5][14][24]

It is noteworthy that the Kayfiyāt of 'Anāṣir depends on their specific Surat Nauiya. This is why, after the nullification of Surat Nauiya, the intrinsic Kayfiyāt of 'Anāṣir also becomes nullified, while the Ṣūrat Naw'iyya (specific form) of Murakkabat (compounds) depends on their Kayfiyāt. This is why, after the change of Kayfiyāt, the Ṣūrat Naw'iyya (specific form) of Murakkabat (compounds) also becomes nullified, and with the establishment of Kayfiyāt, the Surat also remains intact. [5][14][24]

Kayfiyāt (Quality) is an attribute that neither can be divided nor can have any proportion.

Explore Kaifiyat (Qualities) from different perspectives

Unani Medicine is deeply rooted in the concept of **Mizaj (Temperament)** and **Kaifiyat (Qualities)**, which govern the physiological and pathological processes of the human body. The four fundamental qualities—**Hararat (Heat), Barudat (Cold), Rutubat (Moisture), and Yabusat (Dryness)**, play a crucial role in determining the nature of substances, the state of human health, and the effectiveness of treatments. Understanding these qualities is essential for diagnosing diseases, formulating treatments, and maintaining the equilibrium of the human body. The balance of Kaifiyat is central to Unani philosophy, as it influences bodily functions, organ activity, and the nature of diseases. By studying Kaifiyat in depth, Unani scholars have developed a system that integrates dietary habits, herbal treatments, and lifestyle modifications to sustain health and restore balance in case of illness.

Unani medicine classifies physical forms into two fundamental types: **Kamiyat (Quantity) and Kaifiyat (Quality).** Kamiyat, or quantity, precedes Kaifiyat, as the existence of qualities is dependent on the presence of a certain quantity. If there is no quantity, there can be no associated quality. In this context, Kaifiyat refers to specific attributes that define the physical and functional nature of a substance or organism. These qualities are indivisible and cannot be fragmented into smaller parts while retaining their identity. Examples include **heat, coldness, moisture, dryness, color, smell, and taste.** The Kaifiyat of a compound is derived from the combination of the four **Anasir (Elements),** which prepare it to adopt a **Surat Naw'iyya (specific form).** Since temperament determines structure, the variations in the form of compounds arise due to differences in their temperament.[5,24]

Kaifiyat also plays a crucial role in the transformation of substances. The Kaifiyat of an element depends on its **Surat Nauiya (specific structural form).** If the Surat Nauiya is altered or nullified, the intrinsic Kaifiyat of that element also disappears. Conversely, the structural form of compounds depends on their Kaifiyat, meaning that a change in Kaifiyat leads to a transformation in their form. Hence, the integrity of a substance is directly linked to its inherent Kaifiyat.

Kaifiyat can be categorized into **Shabiya (Similar) and Ghair Shabiya (Dissimilar).** For instance, whiteness is similar to white but dissimilar to black. Some qualities remain permanent from birth, such as the blackness of a crow, while others are temporary, like the redness of the face due to embarrassment. These temporary qualities are called **Infaliyat** (reactive qualities). Another category of Kaifiyat is **Nafsani (Mental or Psychological) qualities**, which exist in beings with intellect. These include pain, pleasure, emotions, and behaviors. A long-lasting Nafsani Kaifiyat is referred to as **Malika (Habit),** while a temporary one is called **Hal (State).**[5,24,36]

According to Unani scholars such as **Jalinoos (Galen)** and **Buqrat (Hippocrates),** Kaifiyat directly influences both the internal and external aspects of the body. The fundamental Kaifiyat—**Heat, Cold, Moisture, and Dryness**—affect physiological functions, whereas other Kaifiyat, such as **vision, smell, hearing, and taste,** do not alter the essential nature of the body but influence perception. The Unani perspective holds that all bodily transformations and functions arise due to the interplay of these fundamental qualities.

Kaifiyat defines the behavior, function, and interactions of bodily organs, substances, and external influences. The **four primary Kaifiyat—Hararat, Barudat, Rutubat, and**

Yabusat, govern the balance of health and disease. Each organ, humor (**Khilṭ**), and temperament (**Mizāj**) possess a unique combination of these qualities that determine their normal physiological functions. If these qualities become imbalanced, disease manifests. The **Mizaj** of an individual is the overall balance of Kaifiyat in their body, shaping their physical and mental characteristics.

The faculties (**Quwā**) of the body, such as **Quwwat Jādhiba (Power of Absorption), Quwwat Māsika (Power of Retention), Quwwat Hāḍima wa Mughayyira (Power of Digestion and Transformation),** and **Quwwat Dāfi'a (Power of Expulsion),** all rely on specific Kaifiyat for their proper function. For example, the stomach's hot and moist temperament enables efficient digestion, while the liver's hot and dry nature supports metabolism. If any of these qualities become **Ghayr Mu'tadil (imbalanced),** disorders such as **indigestion, acidity, or jaundice** arise.

When Kaifiyat becomes excessive or deficient, it results in **Sū'-i-Mizāj (Abnormal Temperament).** These abnormalities are classified into:

1. **Sū'-i-Mizāj Ḥārr (Excess Heat):** Caused by spicy foods, hot climates, or emotional stress, leading to symptoms like inflammation, fever, and excessive thirst. Cooling foods like cucumber and rose water help restore balance.

2. **Sū'-i-Mizāj Bārid (Excess Cold):** Caused by cold foods, sedentary lifestyle, or cold weather, leading to weak digestion, lethargy, and poor circulation.

Warming foods like ginger and black pepper are recommended.

3. **Sū'-i-Mizāj Raṭb (Excess Moisture):** Results from high liquid intake and humid conditions, causing phlegm buildup, obesity, and sluggishness. Dry foods like barley and nuts help reduce excess moisture.

4. **Sū'-i-Mizāj Yābis (Excess Dryness):** Caused by dehydration and dry climates, leading to dry skin, constipation, and brittle hair. Moist foods like honey and olive oil help restore balance.

Diseases in Unani medicine are classified as **Māddī (Material) and Ghayr Māddī (non-material).** Material diseases arise from excess or deficient humors (**Khilṭ**), while non-material diseases result from an imbalance in Kaifiyat without changes in humor levels. Fever (**Hummā**) is a prime example of Kaifiyat imbalance. **Excess Hararat (Heat)** leads to high fever and inflammation, requiring cooling treatments. **Excess Barudat (Cold)** causes chills and weakness, needing warming therapies. **Excess Rutubat (Moisture)** results in congestion and sluggish digestion, while **excess Yabusat (Dryness)** leads to dehydration and dry cough.

Kaifiyat is the cornerstone of health in Unani medicine, influencing an individual's temperament, organ function, and disease susceptibility. A balanced Kaifiyat ensures optimal digestion, metabolism, and overall well-being, while its imbalance leads to disease. Unani scholars emphasize that the **body functions as an interconnected system of qualities,** and any disturbance in this equilibrium manifests as illness. By regulating **Hararat, Barudat, Rutubat, and Yabusat** through proper diet, lifestyle adjustments, and herbal remedies, one can maintain health and longevity. Unani medicine thus offers a **holistic approach to well-being** by focusing on the balance of Kaifiyat, ensuring harmony between the human body and nature.

Causes that Increases Kayfiyāt:

Causes that Increases Hotness:[(40)]

- Actions that ignite body heat, such as creating a flame by rubbing stones together.
- Prolonged exposure to hot and moderate air and sunlight.
- Infections within the body that can be exacerbated by even a slight increase in temperature.
- Sudda (Obstruction) in the body's channels.
- Consumption of Har medicines and foods like antidotes, garlic, onion, mustard, honey, etc.
- Intense hunger and thirst.
- Grief and sorrow (prolonged wakefulness increases body heat.

- Anger and rage (stress increases body heat).
- Moderate food and medicine, balanced massage and movement, moderate baths, balanced sleep and wakefulness, balanced anger and joy, cold weather, infection.

Causes that Increases Coldness:[(40)]

Coldness increases through the opposite of the factors that increase Hotness (heat). For instance:

- Excessive movement or rest.
- Excessive eating or drinking, or eating too little.
- Consumption of cold foods and medicines.
- Very hot air, Hot and hard compresses, Bathing in hot water.
- Blocked pores due to excessive cold, Excessive Istafragh.
- Use of potentially or actually cold ointments, Blockages.
- Frequent sexual intercourse, Extreme grief, Extreme joy.
- Great pleasure like sexual intercourse, Raw materials.
- Activities that increase coldness.

Causes that Increases Moistness (Ruṭūbat):[40]

- Comfort and rest, Humid air, sleeping a lot after eating.
- Excessive consumption of Ratab foods and drinks.
- Avoiding Istifrāgh(purging), Istifrāgh Safra,
- Moderate baths after eating, Balanced happiness.
- Cold compresses, slightly warm air, slightly cold air.
- Lack of movement and exercise.

Causes that Increases Dryness (Yubūsat): [40]

Opposite of the causes which increases *Moistness (Ruṭūbat)*, such as:

- Excessive movement, wakefulness, Istifrāgh(purging).
- Continuous hard fatigue, less eating and drinking.
- Consumption of dry foods and drinks, Continuous grief.
- Frequent bathing with astringent water.
- Dryness under the influence of hot air.
- Sudda (Obstructions), Hot compresses.
- Staying in the bath for a long time.
- Extreme anger.

Characteristics of the Kayfiyāt Arba'a:[1, 5,15,24,36,40]

1-Hararat (HOTNESS)

Heat is one of the most powerful and necessary forces in nature, playing a fundamental role in shaping the world around us. It influences how substances change, how living beings function, and how energy is transferred across various systems. The presence of heat allows for growth, movement, and transformation, but excessive heat can also lead to destruction. Understanding the characteristics of heat helps us appreciate its importance and manage its effects efficiently in different aspects of life, from science and technology to health and spirituality. Hararat causes Tahallul (dissolution), Creates stimulation, Generates warmth, Creates delicacy, Creates lightness, Causes burning, Spreads out, Causes destruction, Creates openness, Causes dryness evaporation, Scatters, Leads to maturation. Let's more explore Harārat-

1- Heat Melts and Breaks Things Down: Heat has the remarkable ability to break down solid substances, turning them into liquids or gases. When a solid is heated, its molecular bonds weaken, allowing it to transition into a more fluid state. This principle is evident in our daily lives when ice melts into water or when butter softens on warm toast. In cooking, heat is essential for breaking down the tough fibres in food, making it more palatable and digestible. Similarly, industries rely on heat to melt metals, which are then moulded into tools, machines, and jewellery. Even in nature, glaciers and polar ice caps melt due to rising temperatures, affecting sea levels and climate patterns. Heat's capacity to dissolve and transform substances is a crucial factor in physical and chemical processes.

2- Heat Makes Things Soft and Flexible: Heat plays a vital role in making materials softer and easier to shape or use. Many substances that are rigid at low temperatures become pliable when heated. In everyday life, we see this effect when ironing clothes—heat removes wrinkles by relaxing the fabric, Fibers. In metalwork, blacksmiths heat iron and steel to high temperatures, making them malleable enough to be forged into tools and weapons. Similarly, in glassmaking, heat allows artisans to shape molten glass into decorative and functional items. Even in the human body, heat therapy is used to relax stiff muscles, reduce pain, and improve mobility. The ability of heat to create flexibility is essential for various practical and therapeutic applications.

3- Heat Expands and Moves Objects: When heat is applied to a substance, its particles move faster, causing the material to expand. This property is observable in the way hot air balloons rise—the heated air inside the balloon becomes lighter than the cooler air outside, causing it to ascend. In baking, dough rises because heat expands the gases trapped inside, making the bread light and fluffy. In nature, railway tracks expand in hot weather, which is why engineers leave small gaps between them to prevent warping. The expansion caused by heat is also why liquid thermometers work—the liquid inside rises as it expands with temperature changes. This ability of heat to induce movement and expansion is fundamental in thermodynamics and engineering.

4- Heat Spreads and Balances Temperature: Heat naturally flows from a warmer object to a cooler one until both reach an equilibrium. This principle explains why a hot cup of tea gradually cools down as heat dissipates into the surrounding air. In weather systems, heat from the sun warms the earth, creating air circulation patterns that drive wind and climate changes. Cooking relies on this heat transfer—when a frying pan is heated, the heat spreads across its surface, ensuring food is evenly cooked. The human body also regulates temperature through heat distribution—blood circulates warmth throughout the body, while sweating releases excess heat to cool us down. This natural balancing act ensures that energy is efficiently distributed within different systems.

5- Heat Causes Dryness by Removing Moisture: Heat is responsible for the evaporation of water, turning liquids into gases. This effect is seen when wet clothes dry quickly in the sun, as the heat absorbs and removes moisture from the fabric. In agriculture, excessive heat can dry out the soil, making it harder for crops to grow. Cooking also relies on heat-induced dryness—foods like chips and biscuits become crisp as moisture is evaporated during baking. However, excessive heat can cause dehydration in humans, leading to health issues such as dizziness, fatigue, and heatstroke. Managing heat exposure is crucial for maintaining hydration and preventing excessive dryness in both natural and artificial environments.

6- Heat Supports Growth and Development: Heat is essential for life, aiding in growth, development, and reproduction. In plants, warmth accelerates germination and ripening—fruits such as bananas and tomatoes mature faster in warm climates. In the animal kingdom, many species rely on external heat sources to regulate their body temperature, such as reptiles basking in the sun. Human life also depends on heat, babies develop inside their mother's warm womb, and newborns need warmth to survive. Even in industrial applications, heat speeds up chemical reactions that are necessary for producing fertilizers, medicines, and food products. The presence of heat fosters progress and development across multiple domains.

7- Excessive Heat Can Be Destructive: While heat is beneficial, too much of it can cause damage and destruction. Wildfires are a devastating example—excessive heat and dry conditions can ignite massive forest fires that destroy wildlife and ecosystems. Machines and electronic devices can overheat, leading to malfunctions or breakdowns. In human health, prolonged exposure to high temperatures can result in heat exhaustion, dehydration, and burns. Cities with extreme heat conditions experience heatwaves, which can lead to power outages and water shortages. Managing heat through cooling systems, protective clothing, and proper hydration is crucial to prevent these harmful effects.

8- Heat Influences Emotions and Spirituality: Beyond its physical effects, heat also symbolizes energy, passion, and transformation in human emotions and spirituality. When people feel angry, their body temperature often rises, making them "hot-headed." Similarly, feelings of love and warmth are associated with heat, as in the phrase "a warm heart." In many religious and cultural traditions, fire is a symbol of purification, divine power, and enlightenment. Rituals involving candles, lamps, and sacred flames are common across various spiritual practices. This metaphorical connection between heat and emotions highlights its deep-rooted significance in human perception and cultural expressions.

9- Heat Powers Technology and Industry: Industries and modern technology rely heavily on heat to generate energy and drive production. Power plants burn fuel to create steam, which spins turbines to produce electricity. Solar panels harness the heat from the sun to generate clean energy. In the automotive industry, car engines convert fuel into heat energy, enabling movement. Manufacturing processes such as glassmaking, steel production, and ceramic baking require intense heat to shape and strengthen materials. Without the controlled application of heat, modern advancements in engineering, transportation, and energy production would not be possible.

The Balance of Heat: Heat is a force that permeates every aspect of life, enabling transformation, energy transfer, and growth. It facilitates essential processes such as cooking, movement, weather changes, and industrial production. However, excessive heat can lead to destruction, dehydration, and harm, necessitating careful management. Understanding the characteristics of heat allows us to harness its benefits while mitigating its risks. By maintaining a balance, we can use heat effectively to sustain life, advance technology, and promote well-being in both natural and human-made environments.

2-BARUDAT (Coldness)

Coldness is a natural force that reduces energy, slows down movement, and makes things more compact and solid. It is the opposite of heat and plays a fundamental role in shaping the physical world. Coldness affects everything around us, our bodies, water, air, food, machines, and even emotions. It is essential for maintaining balance in nature and has both benefits and drawbacks. While coldness helps preserve food, reduce heat, and provide relief on a hot day, excessive cold can lead to freezing, discomfort, slow movement, and even health problems. By understanding how coldness works in different aspects of life, we can appreciate its effects and learn how to adapt to them efficiently. So main functions of coldness are Slows down movement, Creates coldness. Causes accumulation and freezing, creates density and heaviness, causes lethargy and Compactness, provides calmness, extinguishes heat, gradually causes dryness more explore barudat-

1. Coldness Slows Down Movement and Activity: One of the most noticeable effects of coldness is its ability to slow things down by reducing energy. This is evident in nature, daily life, and technology. In winter, rivers and lakes move sluggishly because cold water becomes thicker and less fluid, reducing its ability to flow smoothly. Snowflakes fall gently because the cold air causes water vapor to freeze into tiny ice crystals, which descend more slowly than raindrops. In the human body, cold temperatures make people feel sleepy and less active as metabolism slows down to conserve energy. Muscles become stiff in winter, making movement more difficult, and hands and feet often feel numb due to reduced blood circulation. The impact of coldness is also visible in machines and technology, as car engines take longer to start in winter due to the thickening of engine oil. Similarly, batteries drain faster in cold conditions because the chemical reactions inside them slow down. Overall, coldness reduces movement, making things slower and less active in various aspects of life.

2. Coldness Causes Accumulation and Freezing: Cold temperatures turn liquids into solids and promote accumulation instead of dispersion. This is evident in daily life, food preservation, and nature. When water is exposed to freezing temperatures, it solidifies into ice, forming frost, snow, and icicles. During winter, snow accumulates on rooftops, trees, and roads, creating a frozen landscape. In food preservation, cold temperatures play a crucial role in extending the shelf life of perishable items. Refrigerators and freezers slow down bacterial growth, keeping food fresh for longer periods. Frozen food can last for months without spoiling because cold inhibits decomposition and microbial activity. In nature, rain transforms into hailstones when exposed to extremely low temperatures, while glaciers form over thousands of years as layers of snow freeze and compact into dense ice masses. Coldness, therefore, acts as a preserving force, ensuring longevity and stability in different environments.

3. Coldness Creates Density and Heaviness: When substances are exposed to cold temperatures, they shrink, become denser, and feel heavier. This principle applies to air, water, and even the human body. Cold air is denser than warm air, which is why it tends to stay near the ground while warm air rises. This is why winter air often feels thick and heavy, making breathing more challenging for some individuals. In water bodies, cold water is heavier than warm water, causing it to sink to the bottom while warmer layers stay at the surface. This phenomenon plays a vital role in ocean currents and weather patterns. Liquids like oil also become thicker and harder to pour in winter due to the increased density caused by coldness. Within the human body, blood circulation slows down in cold temperatures, leading to sluggishness and fatigue. Additionally, joints and muscles tend to feel stiff and compact in winter, making movement more difficult. Coldness thus plays a critical role in increasing density and compactness in both living and non-living systems.

4. Coldness Causes Lethargy and Compactness: Cold temperatures not only slow down physical movement but also lead to a state of lethargy and compactness. People tend to feel more tired and less energetic in winter because their body conserves energy by reducing metabolic activity. Cold hands and feet often indicate sluggish circulation, making movement challenging. In the animal kingdom, many species adapt to extreme cold by entering a state of hibernation. Bears and other animals significantly reduce their body functions during winter to survive with minimal energy consumption. Birds, on the other hand, migrate to warmer regions to escape the harsh effects of cold. Plants also respond to cold temperatures by shedding their leaves and slowing down growth processes to conserve energy. Crops take longer to grow in cold climates compared to warm environments, further demonstrating how coldness limits activity and expansion.

5. Coldness Provides Calmness and Extinguishes Heat: Coldness counteracts heat and provides a cooling effect that can be both refreshing and beneficial. This effect is commonly observed in daily life, temperature control, and medicine. Drinking a cold glass of water on a hot day brings instant relief, while a cool breeze at night promotes relaxation and better sleep. In terms of fire and temperature regulation, water is widely used to cool down hot objects or extinguish flames, demonstrating the power of coldness in neutralizing heat. Air conditioners and refrigerator's function based on this principle, effectively lowering temperatures to create a comfortable environment. In medicine, cold therapy is often used to treat swelling and pain. Ice packs help reduce inflammation and provide relief from injuries by numbing affected areas and slowing blood flow. Cold water can also help bring down fever by drawing excess heat away from the body. Overall, coldness serves as a natural cooling mechanism, providing comfort and maintaining balance in different settings.

6. Coldness Gradually Causes Dryness: Over time, coldness removes moisture from objects, leading to dryness in the environment, food, and the human body. Winter air tends to be dry, causing skin to become rough, cracked, and in need of extra hydration. Snowfall further reduces humidity levels, intensifying dryness in the atmosphere. In food preservation, cold storage prevents moisture buildup, keeping food fresh and dry. Some foods, such as dried fish and meat, are stored in cold, dry conditions to prevent spoilage. Cold temperatures also affect the human body, as dry winter air can cause hair to become brittle and lips to chap. Breathing in cold air can irritate the throat and lead to coughing or dryness in the nasal passages. Thus, while coldness can be useful for preservation, its drying effect can also create challenges that require proper hydration and care.

7. Too Much Cold Can Be Harmful: While coldness has many benefits, excessive cold can create difficulties by freezing water, slowing movement, and causing discomfort. In nature, lakes and rivers freeze in extreme temperatures, disrupting ecosystems and making water inaccessible for animals. Heavy snowfall can block roads and houses, making transportation and daily activities difficult. In the human body, extreme cold can cause frostbite, a condition where skin and underlying tissues freeze, leading to permanent damage. Cold air can also trigger respiratory issues, such as asthma, by irritating the airways. Machines and vehicles are not immune to extreme cold, as car batteries tend to lose charge faster, and water pipes can freeze and burst if not properly insulated. These examples highlight the challenges posed by excessive cold and the need to take protective measures to mitigate its negative effects.

8. Coldness in Human Emotions and Symbolism: Coldness is not just a physical phenomenon; it also carries significant emotional and symbolic meanings. In human behavior, a person who lacks warmth, empathy, or emotional connection is often described as "cold-hearted." Similarly, a "cold silence" during an argument can indicate distance, indifference, or tension between individuals. Symbolically, colours such as blue and white are associated with coldness, representing tranquillity, winter, and calmness. In literature and films, villains are often portrayed with "cold eyes" to emphasize their lack of compassion. These symbolic interpretations of coldness reflect its broader impact on human perception and communication.

Coldness plays a fundamental role in shaping the natural world and human experiences. It slows down movement, reduces energy, and promotes accumulation and preservation. It increases density, provides calmness, and extinguishes heat. Over time, coldness leads to dryness, affecting both living and non-living things. However, excessive cold can also bring discomfort, freezing, and health issues. By understanding coldness, we can harness its benefits for preservation, relaxation, and balance while taking precautions against its potential challenges.

3- Moistness (Ruṭūbat)

Moistness is a natural quality that plays a crucial role in shaping the physical world and maintaining life. It imparts softness, flexibility, smoothness, and adaptability to objects and living beings. Found in water, air, food, plants, and the human body, moisture ensures the hydration, freshness, and vitality of all things. Without moisture, life would not be possible, as water is an essential component of survival for humans, animals, and plants alike. Moist substances are often light and thin, allowing them to flow and spread easily, making them significant in daily activities, nature, and various industries. However, excess moisture can sometimes lead to stickiness, slipperiness, and even structural weakness. Therefore, understanding the balance of moisture is necessary to maintain strength, beauty, and functionality in different aspects of life. Main functions of moistness are Creates softness, the quality of expansion and contraction, causes thinness, easily accepts and releases shapes, Creates smoothness and beauty, Dissolves into vapor with heat. Let's explore more about Ruṭūbat-

1. **Moistness Creates Softness and Flexibility**: One of the most important characteristics of moisture is that it makes objects soft, flexible, and capable of expanding or contracting as needed. The presence of moisture prevents dryness, brittleness, and stiffness, ensuring that materials and living tissues remain pliable and adaptable. In nature, moist soil is easy to dig and shape, whereas dry soil becomes hard and cracks under pressure. Similarly, fresh fruits such as oranges and apples are soft and juicy due to their moisture content, but as they lose water, they shrink, wrinkle, and become dry. In the human body, skin that is well-hydrated remains smooth and supple, while dry skin turns rough, irritated, and prone to cracking. Moisture is also essential for maintaining eye comfort, as tears keep the eyes lubricated and prevent dryness that can cause discomfort or vision problems. Additionally, materials such as leather require moisture to remain soft and durable, as dryness leads to cracks and stiffness. Similarly, dough is soft and malleable because of its moisture content, allowing it to be shaped and kneaded, while dry flour remains loose and unable to form any structure. These examples highlight the essential role of

moisture in maintaining softness, elasticity, and adaptability in everyday life.

2- Moist Substances Are Thin and Light: Moist substances generally possess a light, thin, and fluid-like nature, allowing them to spread, flow, and distribute evenly across surfaces. This characteristic makes moisture essential in different fields, including cooking, climate control, and human physiology. In liquids, water is the best example of a thin and light substance, as it spreads quickly when spilled, whereas denser liquids such as oil move slowly and form thick layers. Similarly, fruit juices flow easily and are simple to drink, while heavier liquids like honey take longer to pour and stick to surfaces. Moisture also affects air quality, as humid air tends to feel lighter and allows for easier breathing, whereas excessively dry air can cause irritation in the throat and nasal passages. The presence of moisture in the atmosphere contributes to cloud formation, which later results in rain, ensuring the continuation of the water cycle. Within the human body, moisture plays an essential role in maintaining proper circulation. Blood, which is primarily composed of water, flows smoothly through the veins and arteries, while dehydration can lead to thicker blood, slowing circulation and causing health issues. Similarly, saliva aids in digestion and swallowing, making food consumption more comfortable, whereas a dry mouth can lead to discomfort and difficulty in chewing and swallowing. These properties of moisture are thinness, lightness, and its ability to spread, make it a key factor in both natural and biological processes.

3- Moistness Helps Things Accept and Change Shape Easily: Moisture increases the adaptability of objects, making them more receptive to shaping, moulding, and bending without breaking. This characteristic is evident in various aspects of daily life, construction, and nature. Wet clothes, for instance, can be folded, twisted, or shaped more easily than dry clothes, which become stiff and rigid. Similarly, dough, due to its moisture content, can be moulded into different forms, whereas dry flour remains loose and unable to hold a shape. In construction and art, moisture plays an essential role in shaping materials. Clay, when wet, is soft and can be sculpted into intricate designs, but once it dries, it hardens and loses its ability to be reshaped. Similarly, cement remains flexible and adaptable when mixed with water, allowing workers to Mold it into desired forms, but once it sets and dries, it becomes a solid structure. Plants also demonstrate this principle, as green leaves filled with moisture are flexible and can bend without breaking, while dry leaves become brittle and easily crumble. In trees, the presence of moisture within the trunk ensures strength and flexibility, while dried-out trees become weak and prone to breaking. Moistness, therefore, is vital in making objects pliable, adaptable, and easily shaped for various applications.

4- Moistness Creates Smoothness and Enhances Beauty: Moisture is closely linked to smoothness, freshness, and beauty. It enhances the appearance and texture of objects, making them more visually appealing and pleasant to touch. In the human body, hydrated skin appears soft, glowing, and healthy, whereas dry skin looks dull and rough. Hair, too, benefits from moisture, as hydrated hair remains shiny, smooth, and strong, while dry hair becomes frizzy and prone to breakage. In nature, green leaves and fresh plants look vibrant and full of life because of their moisture content, while dried leaves lose their shine and appear withered. Water bodies such as rivers, lakes, and ponds contribute to the beauty of landscapes, but when they dry up, they turn into barren, cracked land. Food and beverages also rely on moisture for an appealing texture and taste. Fresh fruits and vegetables are plump and juicy, while dried ones shrink and become rough. A moist cake is soft, delicious, and easy to eat, whereas an overly dry cake crumbles and lacks the desired texture. These examples illustrate how moisture contributes to maintaining smoothness, freshness, and attractiveness in both living and non-living things.

5- Moisture Turns into Vapor with Heat: One of the dynamic properties of moisture is its ability to evaporate and turn into vapor when exposed to heat. This transformation plays a crucial role in cooling mechanisms, weather patterns, and various everyday activities. In nature, puddles of water disappear after exposure to sunlight as heat causes evaporation. This principle is responsible for cloud formation, where water vapor rises into the sky, later condensing into rain. The human body relies on moisture evaporation for temperature regulation, as sweating helps to cool the skin by releasing moisture into the air. Another example is seen in cooking and drying processes—boiling water produces steam, which is used in food preparation, while wet clothes dry faster when left in the sun. Moisture evaporation is an essential phenomenon that influences environmental and biological systems, helping to maintain balance in nature and human life.

6- Too Much Moisture Can Cause Stickiness and Weakness: While moisture is necessary for life and flexibility, excessive moisture can lead to problems such as stickiness, slipperiness, and structural instability. In daily life, excessive sweating can make the body feel sticky and uncomfortable. Roads become dangerously slippery when wet, increasing the risk of accidents. In food preservation, too much moisture can cause bread to become soggy and mouldy, making it unappetizing. Paper exposed to excess humidity absorbs moisture, weakening its structure and making it more likely to tear. Similarly, buildings and wooden structures are affected by excessive moisture, as damp walls encourage Mold growth, while wooden furniture swells and warps due to moisture absorption. Therefore, while moisture is beneficial, maintaining an appropriate balance is essential to prevent its negative effects.

7: Moistness in Human Emotions and Symbolism: Beyond its physical properties, moistness also holds symbolic meanings in human emotions, literature, and culture. Tears, which are a form of moisture, represent deep emotions such as sadness, joy, or relief. People who are adaptable and easy-going are often compared to water, symbolizing their ability to adjust to different situations. Water is universally seen as a symbol of life, renewal, and purification, reflecting its fundamental role in sustaining existence. In literature and poetry, rain is often associated with transformation, new beginnings, and emotional depth. Moistness, therefore, is not only a physical characteristic but also a metaphor for fluidity, adaptability, and emotional expression.

So, Moistness is one of the most essential qualities in nature and life. It plays a vital role in maintaining softness, flexibility, and smoothness, allowing objects and living beings to function optimally. It enables adaptation, enhances beauty, and contributes to essential biological and environmental processes. However, too much moisture can lead to stickiness and instability. By understanding the significance of moisture, we can better appreciate its role in hydration, comfort, and beauty while maintaining a balance to prevent excess or deficiency.

4- Dryness (Yubūsat)

Dryness (Yubūsat) is a fundamental natural quality that affects the texture, structure, and stability of objects, living beings, and even emotions. It is the opposite of moisture and plays a significant role in shaping the physical properties of materials, the preservation of food, the strength of construction, and the resilience of the human body. Dryness makes things rough, dense, hard, and compact, reducing flexibility but adding durability. While dryness ensures strength and long-lasting stability, excessive dryness can lead to cracking, stiffness, and brittleness, which may be undesirable in some cases. By observing nature, daily life, and various industries, we can see how dryness plays a crucial role and why maintaining a balance between dryness and moisture is essential for both living and non-living things.

One of the primary characteristics of dryness is that it **creates roughness and density.** When moisture is removed from an object, it becomes rougher, firmer, and more resistant to external forces. For instance, dry soil is hard and difficult to dig, whereas moist soil remains soft and easy to cultivate. In the natural world, dry tree bark is rough and rigid, protecting the inner layers of the tree, while fresh bark is more flexible and smoother. The same principle applies to the human body, dry skin feels rough, can crack easily, and requires hydration to remain smooth and elastic. Similarly, dry lips become chapped and uncomfortable, requiring lip balm to restore moisture. In materials and objects, rough sandpaper is effective for smoothing surfaces due to its dryness, while a dry towel absorbs water better than a wet one because it has more capacity to take in moisture. This illustrates how dryness enhances the firmness and density of objects, making them more resistant to change.

Another important effect of dryness is that it **causes hardness and compactness.** As moisture disappears, objects become more solid and rigid but lose their flexibility. In nature, wood hardens as it dries, making it strong and durable for construction. Freshly cut wood contains moisture, which keeps it soft and pliable, but as it dries, it becomes a sturdy material ideal for building houses and furniture. Similarly, dried leaves become stiff and brittle, whereas fresh leaves retain their flexibility and can bend without breaking. In the realm of food, dry bread becomes hard and difficult to chew, while fresh bread is soft and easy to eat. Dried meat, though it lasts longer due to moisture removal, becomes tough and requires cooking or soaking to regain some softness. In construction, materials like bricks and cement must be thoroughly dried before use because their dryness ensures strength, stability, and durability. Dryness contributes to the toughness of materials, but excessive dryness can reduce adaptability and make objects more prone to breakage under extreme stress.

An essential characteristic of dryness is that dry objects do **not change shape easily**. When an object loses moisture, it becomes rigid and maintains its structure permanently. A dry clay pot, for instance, retains its shape indefinitely, whereas wet clay can be moulded into different forms before drying. Similarly, a dry sponge remains firm, while a wet sponge becomes soft and can be squeezed easily. This phenomenon is also evident in fabrics and clothing—dry fabric is stiff and structured, whereas damp fabric is more flexible and can be adjusted effortlessly. The process of ironing clothes removes moisture, making them crisp and giving them a well-defined structure. In nature, mountains and rocks hold their shape for thousands of years due to their dryness, whereas wet mud remains pliable and can be reshaped by external forces. Dryness, therefore, ensures stability and structural integrity but at the cost of flexibility and adaptability.

One of the most valuable aspects of dryness is that it **enhances strength and durability**. While moisture contributes to softness and flexibility, dryness plays a crucial role in making objects long-lasting and stable. In construction, materials such as bricks, concrete, and cement must be completely dry before being used to build strong structures. Wooden furniture needs to be properly dried to prevent bending, warping, or rotting. In the food industry, drying is an essential method of preservation. Grains, spices, and dried fruits last much longer because the removal of moisture prevents the growth of bacteria, Mold, and fungi. Nuts and seeds are stored in dry conditions to maintain their crisp texture and nutritional value. In the human body, bones are dry and rigid, giving structure and support to the body. Hair, when dry, retains its strength, but excessive dryness can make it brittle and more prone to breakage. These examples highlight the significance of dryness in adding longevity and endurance to various objects and living beings.

However, while dryness is beneficial, too much of it can lead to cracking, weakness, and discomfort. In nature, droughts occur when there is a prolonged absence of moisture in the soil, making it difficult for plants to grow and sustain life. Dry tree branches snap easily, whereas fresh ones bend under pressure without breaking. In the human body, excessive dryness of the skin leads to cracks, irritation, and discomfort, requiring moisturizers and oils to restore hydration. A dry throat causes coughing and soreness, which is often relieved by drinking water. In construction and materials, over-dried bricks can become brittle and may crack under pressure, compromising the integrity of a structure. Similarly, wood that is excessively dry may splinter and break instead of maintaining its usual strength. These instances demonstrate that while dryness is necessary for stability, an excess of it can result in fragility and deterioration, emphasizing the need for balance.

Interestingly, dryness is not limited to physical objects, it also extends to human emotions and symbolic meanings. Dryness is often associated with a lack of emotion, excitement, or vitality. In human behaviour, a person who is unemotional or indifferent is sometimes described as "dry" or "cold-hearted." A dry conversation lacks enthusiasm, engagement, or depth, making it dull and uninteresting. Symbolically, deserts, which are extremely dry landscapes, represent isolation, emptiness, and hardship. In literature and poetry, dryness is often used as a metaphor for aging, stagnation, or the absence of life and energy. Cultures around the world associate dryness with solitude, stability, and, at times, lifelessness. This symbolic dimension of dryness shows how it influences not only the physical world but also human perception and emotional states.

In conclusion, dryness is a fundamental quality that plays a crucial role in shaping the natural world, human life, and various industries. It creates roughness and density, making objects firm and durable. It enhances hardness and compactness, ensuring strength and stability. Dry objects retain their shape permanently, making them ideal for construction and preservation. Dryness is vital for food storage, building materials, and bodily strength, but excessive dryness can lead to cracking, brittleness, and discomfort. Moreover, dryness extends beyond the physical realm into human emotions, symbolizing stability, emptiness, or lack of vibrancy. By understanding the effects of dryness, we can learn to maintain the right balance between dryness and moisture to optimize health, comfort, and longevity in different aspects of life. Whether in nature, daily activities, medicine, or emotions, dryness remains an influential force that must be carefully managed to ensure overall well-being and functionality.

The **cause of existence** is a deep question that asks why anything exists instead of nothing. Different people have different answers to this.

Some philosophers say existence is just the way things are and does not need a reason. Others believe everything must have a cause, and we should find out what started it all.

Science explains that the universe began with the **Big Bang**, but it does not fully explain what caused it. Some scientists think the universe may have come from tiny energy changes, but this is still a mystery.

Many religions believe that **God created everything**. In Islam, Allah is called *Al-Khaliq* (The Creator), meaning He made the universe and everything in it. Religious teachings also say that life has a purpose, such as worshipping God, learning, and doing good.

Some spiritual beliefs, like **Sufism**, say that everything is connected to one source. They believe the universe is a reflection of the divine, and understanding existence means understanding ourselves.

No matter which views we follow, the question of why we exist continues to inspire deep thinking and curiosity.

Chapter 8

Difference Among Creatures

"The beauty of creation lies in the uniqueness of each being." *— Rumi*

- **Three types of creation are found in this world viz. Haywānāt (Animals), Nabātāt (Plants), and Jamādāt (Minerals). Haywānāt include humans and animals. Nabātāt include all plants e.g. trees, herbs, shrubs etc. Jamādāt include minerals, stones etc. These three types of things are collectively called Mawālīd Thalātha (three creatures). All these Mawālīd Thalātha are made up of four basic constituents, which are known as Element Arba'a. These Element Arba'a are rûkn 'Ard, rūkn Mā', rükn --Hawā', and rükn Nār.** (8)

The concept of Element started to evolve in Greece with the origin of philosophy as an answer to search for primordial matter. The search for primordial substance (a substance which has existed since time immemorial), was probably started with **Thales**, Thales was born in Miletus, an ancient Greek city. Thales is widely regarded as first philosopher. He was one of the three great philosophers of Milesian school, the other two being Anaximander and Anaximenes. These three philosophers mainly tried to explain origin and structure of the world. All the three agreed on some primordial substance from which everything came into being. But they disagreed on what this substance was? According to **Thales** it was water, according to **Anaximander** it was "apeiron", an infinite, unlimited, eternal, boundless, and indeterminate substance, and according to **Anaximenes** it was air, Later philosophers also gave different views regarding the primordial substance. As knowledge progressed, it was thought that there might be more than one primordial substance. Some thought that there should be two primary substances. [7][16][41][42][43][44]

Perphyreus gave the theory of three primary substances. Later Empedocles gave the theory of four primary substances. This theory became very popular, and its popularity transcended to field of medicine also. According to this theory everything in the universe is made up of four primary matters viz. Ard, Mā', Hawā', and Nār. All these four primary matters have different roles in formation of any substance. The role of rūkn 'Ard is to provide stable shape to things. The role of rūkn Mā' is that it enables things to acquire their required shape due to its moistness (Ruṭūbat). The need of rūkn Nār is in nudj (concoction) and Taltif (lightening) of things. The role of rūkn Hawa' is to make things light and porous. [24]

In the world, Mawālīd Thalātha—minerals, plants, and animals differ significantly not only in form but also in Af'āl (function). Even within animals or the human body, organs differ vastly in both Surat and Fael, despite being composed of the same four 'Anāṣir. This raises the question of why such differences exist if everything is made from the same four 'Anāṣir. [24]

Philosophers from Unani also attribute distinct properties to the Element. It is stated that Nar (fire) is said to be har yabis (hot dry), hawa (air) is said to be har ratab (hot moist), and arz (earth) is said to be barid yabis (cold dry). Element possesses these attributes in their purest form. The driest are Arz, the coldest are Ma, the moistest are Hawaii, and the hottest are Nar. These characteristics give the compounds some unique characteristics. The habitat of animals or plants is determined by the dominance of any one rukn in the composition of the animate. [7][8][16][24]

Earth Element dominance in composition is necessary for terrestrial habitation. Aquatic organisms are those whose makeup is dominated by rukn Ma (water). The dominance of Air Element is also shown in birds. This dominance renders plants and animal's extremophiles in addition to habitation. The organisms known as thermophiles are able to withstand extremely high or low temperatures. The unique constitution of the animals and plants determines how much excess or lack of warmth, water, and air they can tolerate. It goes without saying that organisms that are mostly composed of water cannot exist on land, and vice versa. Certain creatures consist of one, two, or three Element. [24][45]

From a modern scientific viewpoint, the fundamental components for all plants and animals (including humans) are proteins, fats, and carbohydrates. These substances are also derived from the same four 'Anāṣir, suggesting that the theory of composition in Unani medicine is not very different from modern scientific understanding. The differences in the Surat and Af'āl of various entities are due to the varying amounts of these fundamental components combining in different proportions. [24][46]

Zakariya Razi, in his book "Al-Murshid," states that the four 'Anāṣir are the constituents of the bodies of animals, plants, and minerals. Despite that determined types of these bodies, there is considerable variation among individuals, which is due to differences in the quantity of the constituent 'Anāṣir. Physicians believed that when Kaseef (Heavier) 'Anāṣir (water and earth) combine with Lateef (lighter) 'Anāṣir (air and fire), and Har 'Anāṣir mix with Barid 'Anāṣir, the resulting entities come into existence based on the relative proportions of these 'Anāṣir, leading to the dominance of one 'Unṣur (element) in each entity:[8][14][22][32][45]

-**Minerals**: Dominated by the 'Unṣur earth.

Plants: Dominated by the 'Anāṣir water and earth.

-**Animals**: Their movements and actions are influenced by the dominant 'Unṣur (element), affecting their structure, Temperament, diet, habits, actions, and habitat.

Ibn Rushd believed that plants are formed from the primary combination of 'Anāṣir, and animals come into existence from the subsequent combination. There are noticeable differences between mineral, plant, and animal types.

Minerals are inanimate, while plants and animals are living beings. The balanced internal state (Temperament) differentiates one type from another. (29)

According to Ibn Rushd, Element has a primary order in plants and a secondary order in animals. This indicates that plants are the first living things on Earth. Animals must have descended from plants in some way before they began to depend on them for survival. All animals, whether directly or indirectly herbivorous or carnivorous, depend on plants for their survival. Plants are able to survive in soil, water, air, and heat. Plants acquire minerals and water from the earth, gasses from the air, and vital energy for synthesis from the sun. The main dietary ingredients are produced by plants, and herbivorous animals then consume them. Carnivorous animals consume herbivorous ones, and so the chain of assimilative transfer of Element continues. Eaten and utilized Element return to their original sources through dissolution and after death by putrefaction and degradation. (29)

Unani philosophers have identified a certain range of Temperament for a given species, which is between the extremes of maximum and minimum. It is said that this specific Temperament is the species' Temperament. Temperament varies from one limit to the next; this variation is linked to variations in the members of the species' structures and functions. To explain the origin of races, more sub-ranges within a species' range are described. Within a race, a further restricted range is explained to explain an individual, and as an individual's range is further narrowed, the least liberal range for Temperament particular to racial and species members' organs results." The Temperament must be found within the designated ranges of a certain species or race in order to be considered a member.

Anytime this Temperament surpasses the range limit of the species, functional disruptions become incompatible with the member's ability to survive. Other species exist in the spectrum that extends beyond the boundaries of a given species. Numerous species, races, variations, genus, and classes can therefore be descended from the Temperamental modification. Unani philosophers used the term "Temperament" to characterize all structural and functional variations in this context. Any race or species can live as long as the Temperament coexists peacefully with the surrounding environment. In addition to the influence of building blocks, the surrounding environment modifies the Temperament either momentarily or permanently. (26)(34)(47)(48)

A favourable, harmonious situation between a person's milieu and surrounding environment must exist for improved survival. Certain functions are best suited for a particular structure. Every function that comes from a body is ascribed to its Temperament. As a result, functions are flexible within the parameters that separate the two extremes of Temperament. All functions, including neurological functions, fall under the heading of functions. Included are circulatory, reproductive, vegetative, and psychological.

This distinction explains why Temperament has a far wider meaning than disposition. Both psychological and genetic composition could be involved. [11][24]

The variations in structure and function that occur during distinct stages of life cannot be accounted for by a person's genetic, hormonal, or molecular makeup. The incremental alterations in Temperament the cause of the changes seen at various stages of life. Elderly people's Temperament is least conducive to existence; hence they will inevitably pass away naturally. [11][21]

In reference to biodiversity, which is ascribed to both ecology and genetic and environmental variances. Unani philosophers believe that each type of animal and plant has a unique Temperament. The right amount of Element is incorporated, making it the most appropriate quantity for the members of the species to complete their functions. This leads to the formation of the species-specific Temperament. However, no living thing is thought to have fewer than four Element. There are numerous types of arthropods that resemble dry skeletons. Earth Element predominates in these animals, giving them a dry, hard texture. In contrast, the animals of the Annelida order are controlled by moisture, which makes them voluminous and squishy. [26][45][47]

The dominance of a specific rukn and, consequently, the Temperamental quality is also responsible for a particular habit and environment. Because they are Moistness (Ruṭūbat) dominated, aquatic plants and animals receive the greatest amount of nutrition from rukn ma'. Because of this, they are unable to withstand dry conditions, which significantly changes their Temperament. Eventually, dominance of Earth Element becomes necessary for terrestrial life, and all terrestrial creatures and plants have hotter Temperament than watery dwellers; this is why birds are able to fly, as Air Element dominates in determining Temperament. The lightness of the birds is caused by this hawa dominance. The excessive Hotness of thermophilic animals and plants can be attributed to the prevalence of Fire Element in these organisms. The dominance of Coldness due to exposure to cold environments is credited with causing hibernation; as a result, those animals hibernate in the winter to maintain a minimally normal level of heat and to prevent Temperamental deviation. [(5)(21)(47)]

Every animal's body is designed by nature to fulfil its unique set of traits and purposes. For instance, a lion is a hunting animal that is big and heavy, with canine fangs and keen nails; as such, it possesses courage, boldness, and bravery. In contrast, the rabbit is frightened and cowardly since it is light and feeble. The organs of different Quwa (faculties) are formed with different essences and forms. The difference depends on how one chooses to interpret the functions that come from their Quwwat. Man, for instance, possesses two hands with which he may execute intricate and skilful tasks. Even hands have numerous fingers that vary in size and form depending on what can be removed. [(3)(5)(33)(49)(50)]

Camels can walk on sand more easily because of their huge feet. For this reason, their feet are padded as well. They can open and close their nostrils to keep sand out of their noses. They also have lengthy eyelashes to keep sand out of their eyes. Since food isn't always available in deserts, camels have developed a hump in which they store fat, which they then use to generate energy when needed. [51][52][53]

Characteristics of Living and Non-living Entities: Living Entities (Plants and Animals) possess cellular structure, perform respiration, have sensory perception and cognition, excrete waste products, Have the ability to move. Non-living Entities (Minerals): Lack the above characteristics.

Plants and animals also differ from each other due to factors contributing to their unique balanced internal state. Plants prepare their food through photosynthesis whereas animals Depend on others for food. Cellular structure, respiration, and growth processes are also different in both of them. Differences in chromosome numbers are a significant factor in distinguishing various animal species like Frog has 26 chromosomes, Mouse-40 chromosomes, Cat-38 chromosomes, Dog-78 chromosomes, Human-46 chromosomes, Cow-60 chromosomes, Gorilla-48 chromosomes and Monkey has 42 chromosomes. This variation in chromosome numbers is a fundamental reason for the diversity among animal species.

According to Unani system of medicine, main difference between animals and plants are different composition of Umoor. The Akhlāṭ (Humors), Aza, Af‘āl (*Nafsāni* and *Ḥaywāniyya)* and Arwah (*Nafsān* and *Ḥaywāni*) are related to animals only. But they are absent in plants. [23][47]

According to **Ibn Rushd**, there are numerous traits that influence an animal's temperament. While some of them are terrestrial, others are aquatic. Because Rukn-e-Ma is dominant, aquatic creatures are cold and wet, whereas terrestrial species are hot and dry. While some animals walk. Birds have the dominance of Rukn-e-Hawa compared to walking animals, and walking creatures that have the dominance of Rukn-e-Ard. Similar to how some animals have blood and others do not, animals with blood are warm and wet while those without blood are chilly and dry due to Rukn-e-Ard's domination. In the same way, certain species breathe while others do not. It is heated for those who breathe and chilly for those who do not. Certain animals have a hot and humid temperament, which makes them swift and hardworking; in contrast, sluggish moving animals are cold due to Rukn-e-Ard dominance. [(29)(24)(45)]

Animal temperament varies based on eating habits as well. Rakn-e-Nar dominates carnivorous animals, which are hot and cold. But animals that are herbivorous such as goats, cows, hens, etc are moderate. Large-bodied terrestrial animals possess more Rukn-e-Ard, whereas smaller animals possess less of it. Larger aquatic species have higher levels of Rukn-e-Ma, whereas smaller aquatic creatures have lower levels. Rukn-e-Ard is dominated by animals with hard bones, hooves, horns, scales, and feathers. Since brave animals possess Quwat-e-fadila of Rukn-e-Hawa and Rukn-e-Nār, they have a heated temperament. Animal cowards are cold. While certain animals, like camels, are found in hot countries, the majority of them are cold and hot. Certain animals, like polar bears, are unique to colder climates. Different species have varied temperaments depending on their environment, water, and pasture, for example. Fish found in rocky areas have a Lateef temperament and produce less waste than fish found in muddy water. (29)(24)(45)

Physicians have provided detailed descriptions of the characteristics of plants, including their growth, structure, temperament, and roles in relation to dominant Rukn. There is a dominant Rukn in plants. Earth and water are ruled by plants. For this reason, they are immobile and stay in one spot. Through the roots, they get nutrition. For them, root is a mouth. When plants germinate, they emerge from the earth and grow upward because they contain Rukn-e-Nār. Since the sky is the natural home of fire, this helps explain why these plants grow upward but stay stationary on one location because of the dominance of water and earth. In contrast, creepers contain less Rukn-e-Nār. (14)

Plants that grow in water will wither away if we try to grow them on land because they have a dominance of water and get their nutrients from it. There are two types of plants: complete and incomplete. Incomplete plants lack flowers and leaves and have a dominance of moisture (algae) or earth (champignon). Complete plants grow on moderate hills because they are porous and receive both heat and moisture. Additionally, these plants move as a result of the breezes. In a similar vein, certain plants are cultivated while others are native. Rukn-e-Ma is dominated in cultivated plants; some grow slowly, while others develop swiftly. In contrast to plants growing slowly and having dominance of Rukn-e-Ard, those growing swiftly have dominance of Rukn-e-Ma and Rukn-e-Hawa and have fewer nodes overall. Plants with a predominance of dryness and Rukn-e-Ard reproduce slowly. Rukn-e-Ard's dominance is the reason why certain plants have more thorns and nodes than others. The plants with moderately sized flowers and leaves, and the plants without any flowers or leaves that are either watery or earthy. (29)

Those animals which sniff without breathing have stronger Hiss-e-Shamma than those animals who sniff with breathing. The animals having lesser complicated intestine are poisonous. There are many animals devoid of blood while blooded animals must have respiratory mechanism. Warm-blooded animals (endotherms), such as mammals and birds, rely heavily on respiration to maintain a constant body temperature. Their metabolic processes are highly active, producing heat that helps keep their body warm regardless of the external environment. This high metabolic rate requires a greater oxygen intake, making efficient respiration essential for their survival. In contrast, cold-blooded animals (ectotherms), like reptiles, amphibians, and fish, do not use metabolic heat to regulate their body temperature. Instead, they depend on external environmental conditions to control their body temperature, which means their metabolic rate and oxygen demand are generally lower. Therefore, respiration in cold-blooded animals plays a less pivotal role in temperature regulation compared to warm-blooded animals. [29]

Animals that detect scents without actively "breathing" through a nose tend to have a more specialized and powerful sense of smell, often related to their unique sensory structures. For instance, insects like ants and honeybees possess specialized antennae equipped with highly sensitive olfactory receptors. These receptors can detect pheromones and other chemicals in the environment without the need for the inhaling process, allowing them to identify even minute concentrations of scents. [29]

This heightened sense, often called quwwat al-shamma (the sense of smell), is crucial for their survival, guiding behaviors such as finding food, locating mates, and navigating their environment. In contrast, animals that sniff while breathing, such as mammals, rely on their nasal passages to bring scent molecules into contact with olfactory receptors, which may not be as sensitive to certain chemical cues as the antennae of insects. [29]

The temperament of humans is considered an ideal temperament in comparison to other species. When examining the temperament of humans alongside that of various animals, it reflects a balance that approaches motadil haqeeqi. Similarly, the temperament of animals in relation to plants and the temperament of plants compared to minerals also illustrate this concept of equilibrium, highlighting a harmonious state across these different categories. [5] [29

Uniqueness of Human Creation:

This world is a macrocosm, and humans are the summary and resemblance of this macrocosm. Humans are the only creatures with senses and movement like animals, growth and hairlike plants. They have bones and flesh like stones, and intellect, thoughts, and a rational soul like angels. The veins of their blood are like rivers and streams, and they obtain food like animals, birds, and fish. Like electricity, rays emit from their eyes, making them similar to the sun and planets due to their vision and senses. Because of all these similarities, humans are called the microcosm. The Creator made humans in the best form, and only humans possess the power of contemplation; hence, acquiring knowledge has been made obligatory for them. This way, through their knowledge, consciousness, reflection, reasoning, and experience, they can understand the logical coherence between the creation of the universe, other creatures, environments, and conditions, and connect with the mysteries within. (14)

Humans are unique among all creations, and all the blessings of this world are made for humans. The concept of partial perception is attributed to the Quwwat wahima (faculty of imagination) . Ancient scholars believed that humans possess reason, unlike animals, which are devoid of it. Humans perceive both universals and particulars, while animals only perceive particulars. Humans have both imagination and intellect, while animals only have imagination. Human intellect *Qawwal 'Aquila* is related to the Nafs-e-Natiqa (rational soul), which perceives universals. Philosophers argue that mental faculties perceive only specific meanings, while the comprehension of universal concepts comes from a higher faculty, known as the *Quwwat 'Āqila*. Like humans, animals have the faculty of imagination, enabling them to recognize friends, enemies, benefits, and harms. They strive to avoid harmful things and obtain beneficial ones. [(5)(22)(24)(29)]

Humans are unique because of our advanced intelligence, which allows us to think, solve problems, and create in ways other species cannot. We have complex languages for expressing ideas and emotions, and we can reflect on ourselves and our purpose, which leads to philosophies and a search for meaning. Our creativity and ability to use tools and technology help us shape the world, from inventing basic tools to creating modern innovations like AI.

We also stand out because of our deep emotions, empathy, and ability to form strong social bonds. Humans create art, music, and literature to express themselves and explore beauty. Unlike other species, we adapt to almost any environment through creativity and innovation, building cultures, civilizations, and global connections that make us truly unique.

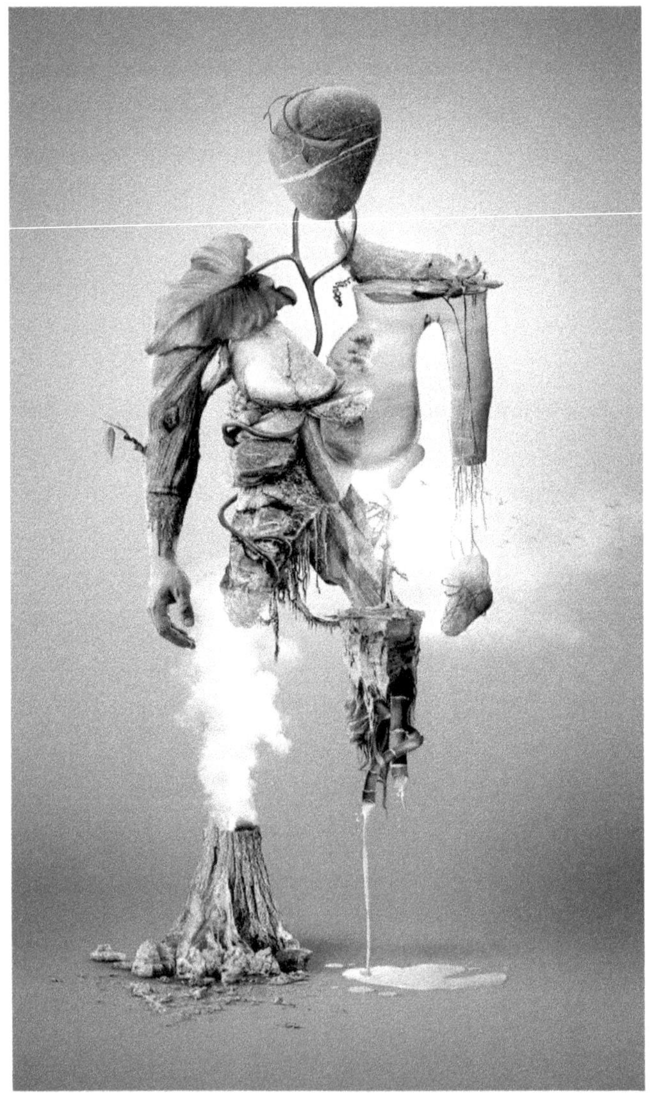

Chapter 9

Evolution and Structural Adaptation

"The only constant in life is change." —
Heraclitus

The idea of evolution and adaptation has changed over time. Ancient Greek philosophers like Aristotle believed that species were fixed, while others suggested that living things might change. During the Middle Ages, most people thought that species were created in their present form and did not evolve.

In the 18th century, scientists like **Linnaeus** and Buffon studied the relationships between species. Lamarck suggested that organisms could develop new traits during their lifetime and pass them on, but this idea was later proven incorrect.

The real breakthrough came with **Charles Darwin** in the 19th century. After studying plants and animals on the Galápagos Islands, he developed the theory of natural selection. This means that organisms with useful traits survive, reproduce, and pass those traits to the next generation. Around the same time, Alfred Wallace also proposed a similar idea.

In the 20th century, genetics helped explain evolution. **Mendel's** work on heredity showed how traits are passed down, and the discovery of DNA proved how genes change over time. Fossils also provided evidence of evolution, showing how species evolved over millions of years.

Today, scientists continue to study evolution through genetics, fossils, and even genetic engineering. Evolution is an ongoing process, shaping life on Earth for the future.

Human evolution is the process by which human beings developed from earlier primates through a series of changes over millions of years. This process involves physical, genetic, and behavioural changes that eventually led to the emergence of modern Homo sapiens.[135]

1. Early Primates (65 million Years Ago): Humans share a common ancestor with modern primates like chimpanzees, gorillas, and orangutans. This ancestor lived around 65 million years ago, shortly after the extinction of dinosaurs. Early primates were small, tree-dwelling creatures with traits like grasping hands and forward-facing eyes, which helped them navigate through trees and see in 3D.

2. Australopithecus (4 to 2 million Years Ago): Around 4 million years ago, a genus called *Australopithecus* emerged. These early hominins were bipedal (walked on two legs) but still had features like long arms and a small brain, similar to apes. *Australopithecus afarensis* is one of the most famous species in this genus, with "Lucy," one of the best-preserved fossils, being an example. These early humans lived in Africa and likely used basic tools.

3. Homo habilis (2.4 to 1.4 million Years Ago): The genus *Homo* emerged with *Homo habilis*, often considered the first true human. They had a larger brain than *Australopithecus* and made simple stone tools. *Homo habilis* likely scavenged meat and used tools to cut through animal carcasses, marking the beginning of more complex behaviours.

4. Homo erectus (1.9 million to 110,000 Years Ago): *Homo erectus* was a significant step in human evolution. They had a larger brain, were fully bipedal, and began to use fire for cooking and warmth. *Homo erectus* was also the first human species to migrate out of Africa, reaching parts of Asia and Europe. Their tools became more sophisticated, and they likely hunted large animals.

5. Neanderthals (400,000 to 40,000 Years Ago): Neanderthals (*Homo neanderthalensis*) were closely related to modern humans and lived in Europe and western Asia. They had a robust physique, larger brains than modern humans, and were skilled hunters. Neanderthals made tools, controlled fire, and possibly had symbolic or ritualistic behaviours, such as burying their dead. There is evidence that Neanderthals interbred with early *Homo sapiens*, contributing to the genetic makeup of some modern human populations.

6. Homo sapiens (300,000 Years Ago to Present): *Homo sapiens*, or modern humans, evolved in Africa around 300,000 years ago. They had a larger brain and more advanced cognitive abilities than their predecessors, allowing for complex language, art, and culture. Early *Homo sapiens* spread out of Africa in waves, replacing or interbreeding with other human species like the

Neanderthals and Denisovans. Over time, *Homo sapiens* developed advanced tools, agriculture, and social structures, ultimately leading to the development of civilizations.

Human evolution is a long and complex process that spans millions of years, with early hominins gradually evolving into modern humans. Key milestones in this process include the development of bipedalism, larger brains, and the ability to create and use tools. Today, *Homo sapiens* are the only surviving species of the genus *Homo*, but our evolutionary history is a testament to the long path that led to our existence

Animals have different body parts that help them live and survive in their environments. For example, animals like lions and wolves have sharp teeth to tear meat, while cows and camels have flat teeth to grind plants. Camels are unique because they don't have upper front teeth; instead, they use a hard part of their mouth to crush food. Animals like humans and bears have both sharp and flat teeth because they eat both plants and meat.

Different animals also have different kinds of stomachs. Cows, deer, and camels have more than one stomach, which helps them slowly digest tough plants. Animals like humans, dogs, and cats have just one stomach, which works faster. Birds like chickens and pigeons have a special part called a gizzard that grinds up food since they don't have teeth. This means animals with many stomachs can eat rough plants, while meat-eaters need quick digestion for fast energy.

Animals move in different ways depending on their legs or lack of them. Horses and dogs have strong legs for running, while humans and birds have two legs—birds use wings to fly. Some animals like snakes and fish don't have legs, so they slither or swim. Running helps animals escape danger or catch food, and birds have light bones that make flying easier. Fish have fins and tails that help them swim smoothly.

Animals also have different types of body coverings. Bears and rabbits have thick fur that keeps them warm. Fish and snakes have scales that protect them from getting hurt and keep their bodies from drying out. Birds have feathers that help them fly and keep warm. This means fur is great for cold weather, scales help in water, and feathers let birds glide through the air.

Animals have special features for defence. Deer and bulls use their horns to fight, while lions and eagles have sharp claws for catching prey or climbing. Some animals, like snakes and scorpions, have venom to deter or kill threats. These adaptations help animals stay safe—strong animals use their horns or claws to fight, while venomous ones make others too afraid to attack.

Breathing also varies among animals. Humans, lions, and eagles use lungs to breathe air, while fish and crabs use gills to extract oxygen from water. Frogs and turtles are unique because they can breathe both in water and on land. This allows land animals to get oxygen from the air, fish to survive underwater, and frogs to switch between breathing with lungs and through their skin.

Animals control their body temperature in different ways. Humans, birds, and lions are warm-blooded, so they keep the same body temperature no matter the weather. Snakes, fish, and frogs are cold-blooded, so their body temperature changes with their surroundings. Warm-blooded animals can live in many places, while cold-blooded ones save energy by matching the weather around them.

Overall, each animal is designed in a special way that helps it survive where it lives. Some have sharp teeth for meat, some have strong legs for running, and others have scales or feathers for protection. Nature has given each animal the perfect tools to thrive in its world.

Evolution and Structural Adaptation of Different Organ

(50,59,116,117,118,119,120,121,122,123)

- **The structural adaptation for Vision**

Eyes have evolved over time to suit different animals' habitats and activities, becoming more complex and improving image quality. Broadly, there are two types of eyes:

1. Compound Eyes: Found in insects, these eyes first appeared about 540 million years ago in trilobites, ancient arthropods. Trilobite eyes were made of calcite, a mineral also found in their shells. Compound eyes consist of many small units called ommatidia, each with its own cornea, lens, and light-detecting cells. Some insects have up to 1,000 ommatidia. These eyes provide a wide field of view and are excellent at detecting fast movements, though they produce low-resolution images. For example, dragonflies use their compound eyes to track and catch fast-moving prey mid-air.

2. Simple Eyes (Camera-Type): Found in most animals, these eyes have a cornea (clear outer layer), iris (controls light), and lens (focuses light onto the retina). The retina contains two types of photoreceptors: 1- Cones: Detect colours and function in bright light. Humans have three types of cones, allowing us to see a range of colours. 2- Rods: Work in low light and detect black and white images. This type of eye is common in animals like mammals, birds, and fish.

Examples of Eye Adaptations:

1. **Earthworms**: Lack complex eyes but have simple photoreceptor cells that detect light and dark. This helps them avoid predators by moving to darker areas and burrowing underground.
2. **Jellyfish**: Most lack complex eyes but use photosensitive cells on their bodies for navigation. Box jellyfish have evolved lens-like eyes that can perceive images, helping them navigate obstacles and hunt.
3. **Starfish**: Have primitive compound eyes at the tips of their arms, lacking lenses and focusing ability. These eyes detect light, dark, and large objects. The number of eyes depends on the number of arms.
4. **Butterflies**: Have a wide field of vision and can detect fast movements. They see ultraviolet light,

allowing them to spot floral patterns invisible to humans.

5. **Spiders**: Have eight simple eyes. The two large front eyes provide clear, colourful images, while six smaller eyes detect motion. Jumping spiders have excellent vision, allowing them to hunt prey and recognize mates.
6. **Octopuses**: Have a single type of photoreceptor sensitive to blue light but use a unique method to perceive colours. Their U-shaped pupil acts as a prism, splitting light into wavelengths, allowing them to "see" colours despite being technically colourblind.
7. **Fish**: Have spherical lenses that give them 360-degree vision. Most fish see colours, and some detect ultraviolet light, helping them find plankton. Sharks, though colourblind, have sharp vision in deep or murky waters.
8. **Frogs**: Focus by moving their lens, unlike humans who adjust the lens's shape. Their eyes are highly sensitive to movement and work well in low light, making them excellent for night vision.
9. **Snakes**: Have poor eyesight and rely on their tongues for smell. Some daytime snakes see shades of blue and green, while nocturnal ones detect ultraviolet light. Pythons, vipers, and boas have heat-sensing pits to locate warm-blooded prey in the dark.

10. **Birds**: Have sharper vision than humans, enabling them to see long distances. They also see ultraviolet light, which helps them find colourful fruits and prey.

Plants and Light Perception: Plants lack eyes but can sense light using photoreceptors that detect direction, quality, and intensity. Phototropism is the process where plants grow toward sunlight, ensuring they capture maximum energy. Roots, in contrast, grow away from light, a behaviour called photophobia. Certain plants can sense specific light frequencies (e.g., 100–500 Hz) to boost activities like seed germination and growth. For example, sunflower stems track the sun across the sky, ensuring optimal light absorption.

- **The structural adaptation for Hearing**

Hearing is a vital sense for animals, helping them detect predators, hunt, navigate, and communicate. In humans, hearing involves several steps. Sound waves enter the external ear, travel to the eardrum, and cause it to vibrate. These vibrations move three tiny bones in the middle ear—malleus, incus, and stapes—which amplify the sound and transfer it to the cochlea in the inner ear. The cochlea, a spiral-shaped structure filled with gel, moves in response to the vibrations, bending tiny hair-like nerves that send signals to the brain, interpreted as sound.

This hearing system is common to mammals, but its origins trace back to ancestral reptiles. While reptiles typically have only one middle ear bone (the stapes or columella), mammals evolved the malleus and incus from reptilian jawbones, allowing them to hear a wider range of sounds.

Different animals have adapted unique hearing mechanisms:

- **Crocodiles** have ears just behind their eyes, which open above water and close when submerged.
- **Snakes** lack external ears but detect ground vibrations through a special apparatus connected to their jawbones.
- **Birds** have ear holes covered by feathers, leading to an eardrum connected to the cochlea via the columella. Their hearing is sensitive to pitch and tone, crucial for communication.
- **Frogs** lack external ears but have eardrums linked to the inner ear by the stapes. Some frogs can also hear through their lungs or mouths.
- **Fish** use otoliths (calcium carbonate structures) in their inner ear. Otoliths detect pressure changes differently from the rest of the fish's body, allowing them to sense sound. These signals are passed to cilia (hair-like cells), which send sound information to the brain.

Marine creatures like octopuses, squids, crabs, lobsters, and shrimp use a statocyst to sense sound. This sac-like structure contains sensitive hairs and mineralized masses, which also help with balance.

Insects have diverse hearing systems:

- **Spiders** sense sound through tiny hair structures (hair sensilla) that vibrate in response to certain frequencies.

- **Mosquitoes** use their antennae to detect sound, which are brush-like and sensitive.
- **Crickets** and **cockroaches** have cephalic organs on their abdomens with fine hairs to detect vibrations.
- **Grasshoppers**, **moths**, and **butterflies** use tympanal organs, thin membranes backed by hair-filled spaces connected to sensory neurons. These organs can be located on their thorax, abdomen, legs, or wings.

Earthworms lack ears but sense vibrations through their skin, helping them avoid predators.

Plants, while lacking ears, can perceive sound vibrations. Mechanosensitive channels in their cells detect vibrations in the soil, enabling them to respond to frequencies between 100–500 Hz. These frequencies promote seed germination, growth, and stronger roots. For example, plant roots show phonotropism, where sound vibrations influence their growth direction. Roots also use subtle clicking sounds to explore soil and locate nutrients.

- **The structural adaptation for Smell and Taste**

The senses of smell and taste help animals interact with their environment, find food, avoid danger, and even communicate. In Humans Smell comes from olfactory sensory neurons, located in a small patch of tissue high inside the nose. These neurons are directly connected to the brain and can detect a wide range of scents. Taste is sensed through taste buds, which are made up of gustatory cells. Taste buds are found not only on the tongue but also on the soft palate, upper oesophagus, cheeks, and epiglottis. Humans can sense sweet, salty, sour, bitter, and umami (Savory) flavours.

1) In Animals

Earthworms: "taste" chemicals in the soil using chemoreceptors spread across their body. This helps them identify safe and nutritious areas to burrow and feed.

Insects

Butterflies: Taste using receptors on their feet. They can detect whether a surface is suitable for laying eggs. They also smell using sensors on their antennae.

Honeybees: Have taste and smell receptors on their antennae, allowing them to identify flowers with nectar.

Spiders: Use sensory organs on their legs and pedipalps to both taste and smell their environment.

Octopuses can taste and smell using sensors located on the suction cups of their arms. This helps them identify food by touching it, even in dark waters.

Fish use nostrils to smell, relying on an internal olfactory system.

Taste buds are found not only on tongues but also on their lips, roof of the mouth, gill arches, and even barbels (whisker-like structures on some fishlike catfish). This helps them detect food in water.

Frogs detect chemical changes in their environment through their nostrils, eyes, and even skin. They use an organ called Jacobson's organ, located on the roof of their mouth, to detect food. Frogs can taste bitter, sweet, sour, and salty Flavors, which helps them avoid toxic or unwanted food.

Birds have taste receptors on their skinny tongues and can detect sweet, sour, and bitter Flavors. This helps them find suitable food, like fruits and seeds. They smell using olfactory sensory neurons, though their sense of smell varies between species. For example, vultures rely heavily on smell to locate carrion.

Snakes don't have traditional taste buds but sense smell using their tongue. When a snake flicks its tongue, it collects scent particles and transfers them to the Jacobson's organ on the roof of its mouth, which processes the scent. This helps snakes track prey or detect predators.

Jellyfish: Detect smells using specialized nerves in their tentacles. **Starfish**: Have chemoreceptors on their skin that help them sense prey, though their sense of smell is weak.

Plants don't have noses or tongues but can still sense and respond to their environment:

Smell in Plants: Plants detect scents using receptors on their cells. These receptors bind to specific volatile molecules, allowing plants to "smell." This ability helps plants:

Communicate: For example, when a plant is attacked by insects, it releases chemical signals that warn nearby plants to prepare their defences.

Attract pollinators: Flowers release fragrances to lure insects or birds for pollination.

Defend themselves: Some plants release distress signals to attract predators of herbivorous insects.

Taste in Plants: Plants "taste" their environment by sensing chemicals in the soil.

Root growth: Roots grow toward areas rich in nutrients by detecting chemical gradients. This is why roots often cluster in nutrient-dense zones.

Carnivorous plants: Some plants, like Venus flytraps and pitcher plants, have evolved to "taste" and digest insects. These plants secrete sugary substances and fragrances to attract insects. Once an insect is trapped, the plant releases enzymes to break it down and absorb nutrients, particularly nitrogen. This adaptation helped carnivorous plants survive in nitrogen-poor soils.

For example, Venus flytraps snap shut when an insect triggers their sensory hairs, while pitcher plants drown insects in a liquid-filled trap and digest them slowly.

So, Smell and taste play vital roles in both animals and plants. While animals use specialized organs like noses, tongues, and sensory receptors, plants rely on chemical sensing through their cells. These abilities enable survival, communication, and adaptation to their environments.

- **The structural adaptation for Mouth**

The mouth plays a vital role in feeding and obtaining energy, which is essential for survival. The design of the mouth varies across different species, depending on their feeding habits and the environment they live in.

In Simple Organisms

Sponges are immobile, but they feed by filtering water. They have tiny pores throughout their body where water flows in, and they expel the water through a larger opening called the osculum. As water moves through, food particles are trapped and absorbed.

Jellyfish have a mouth located at the bottom centre of their umbrella-shaped body. The same mouth is used for both eating and discarding waste. They also use their mouth to squirt water and propel themselves forward.

Starfish have a small mouth at the centre of their underside. They can extend their stomach out of their mouth to partially digest food externally. This is helpful when consuming prey that is too large to swallow whole.

In Complex Organisms

Insects have a variety of mouthparts, which have evolved based on their feeding habits:

- Chewing Mouthparts: Insects like grasshoppers, beetles, ants, and dragonflies have chewing mouthparts for grinding plant material or prey.
- Siphoning Mouthparts: Moths and butterflies use a tube-like mouthpart (proboscis) to suck nectar from flowers.
- Piercing and Sucking Mouthparts: Insects like mosquitoes and leafhoppers use sharp mouthparts to pierce and suck fluids from plants or animals.
- Sponging Mouthparts: Insects like houseflies and spiders secrete saliva onto their food, then suck it back up by capillary action.

Earthworms: do not have teeth, but they have a strong, muscular mouth that helps them burrow into the soil and feed on decayed organic matter, like dead plants and animals.

Octopuses: The mouth of an octopus is located in the centre of its tentacles. They have a sharp, beak-like mouth that helps them crack open the shells of prey, such as crabs.

Fish mouths vary in size, shape, and position depending on their feeding habits:

- **Superior Mouth**: Found in fish that strike from below, like groupers. The lower jaw is larger than the upper jaw, allowing them to catch prey from below.
- **Terminal Mouth**: Fish like tuna and salmon have jaws of equal size, and their mouth is located in the middle of their head. This is useful for chasing and catching prey.
- **Inferior Mouth**: Fishlike catfish have an upper jaw longer than the lower jaw. This mouth is ideal for bottom-feeding fish that eat food from the ocean floor.

Fish also have specialized teeth depending on their diet: Carnivorous Fish have sharp, canine teeth to catch and hold onto prey. Herbivorous Fish may have flat, molar-like teeth to crush plant material.

Frogs have a broad mouth that allows them to swallow whole prey. They have maxillary teeth on the upper jaw and vomerine teeth on the roof of their mouth. These teeth help hold onto prey, but frogs swallow food whole, aided by their eyes pushing the food down.

Snakes have flexible jaws that allow them to swallow large prey. Their teeth are all similar and used for gripping and holding prey. Venomous snakes have long, sharp fangs that are connected to venom sacs to inject poison into prey.

Birds have beaks instead of teeth. The shape of the beak is adapted to the bird's diet:

- Carnivorous Birds, like eagles and owls, have hooked beaks to tear flesh.
- Fruit-eating Birds, like parrots, have sharp, hooked beaks for peeling fruits and crushing nuts.
- Seed-eating Birds, like pigeons and chickens, have conical beaks for cracking seeds.
- Coastal Birds, like pelicans, have long, pointed beaks for catching fish.
- Hummingbirds have long, slender beaks for reaching nectar in flowers.

In Mammals: Mammals have a common dental structure that has evolved to suit their diet. They have four types of teeth:

1. **Incisors**: Flat teeth at the front of the mouth for cutting or slicing food.
2. **Canines**: Pointed teeth next to incisors, used for tearing food.
3. **Premolars**: Found behind canines, used for crushing and grinding food.
4. **Molars**: Located at the back of the mouth, used for grinding and crushing.

Depending on their diet, mammals have different arrangements of these teeth:

- **Herbivores** like cows and deer have flat molars for grinding plants and usually lack canine teeth.
- **Carnivores** like lions and wolves have sharp canines for tearing meat, and their molars are flatter for crushing bones.
- **Omnivores** like humans have a mix of sharp canines for tearing meat and flat molars for grinding plants.

So, the mouth has evolved into many different forms to suit the feeding habits of various animals. Whether it's filtering water, chewing prey, or sucking nectar, the mouth's design is key to survival and energy intake.

➢ The structural adaptation for Respiration

Respiration is the process of taking in oxygen and releasing carbon dioxide, necessary for the survival of living organisms. Over time, the organs responsible for respiration have evolved differently depending on the species and their environment. Here's how various creatures perform respiration:

In Simple Organisms

Sponges don't have specialized respiratory organs. Instead, they rely on diffusion, where oxygen passes directly through their cell membranes. Water flows in through small pores, and oxygen is absorbed directly from the water.

Jellyfish and Starfish: Jellyfish absorb oxygen directly through their skin. Starfish also breathe through diffusion, where oxygen enters directly into their bodies through their skin.

In Complex Organisms

Insects breathe through spiracles, small openings along the sides of their body. These spiracles lead to trachea, tubes that transport air directly to their cells, delivering oxygen and removing carbon dioxide. This system is efficient because it bypasses the need for a blood circulatory system to carry oxygen.

Spiders have book lungs, leaf-like structures in their abdomen that allow gas exchange. These lungs are connected to the outside through small openings, where oxygen is absorbed, and carbon dioxide is released.

Earthworms breathe through their skin, which must remain moist to absorb oxygen. They don't have lungs, so the oxygen enters their body through the skin and into the blood.

Octopuses have gills located inside their bodies. They draw water in through their siphon, a funnel-shaped structure, and push the water out, passing it over their gills to absorb oxygen.

Fish have gills that extract oxygen from water. Water flows in through their mouth, passes over the gills, and exits through openings near their gill covers. Some fish, like sharks, have multiple gills, while bony fish usually have one pair.

Frogs use multiple methods of breathing: Tadpoles have gills and breathe underwater. Adult frogs have lungs for breathing air, and they can also absorb oxygen through their skin when they are in water.

Snakes breathe through their lungs, which are long and thin to fit their body. They take in air through their nostrils and glottis (a small opening at the bottom of their mouth).

Birds have small lungs and special air sacs that allow them to breathe efficiently. These sacs help birds take in fresh air even during exhalation, which is useful for high-altitude flight, ensuring they have a constant supply of oxygen.

Humans breathe through the nose, where air is warmed and humidified before it moves down the throat (pharynx) and windpipe (trachea). From there, it travels into the lungs, passing through branching tubes called bronchi and into smaller tubes called bronchioles. Tiny air sacs called alveoli are where oxygen is exchanged with the blood.

Plant Respiration: Just like animals, plants need oxygen to survive. However, plants don't have a special organ for respiration; it occurs throughout the plant. Here's how plants breathe:

Leaves: Stomata are tiny pores on the surface of leaves that allow gases to enter and exit. These stomata are controlled by guard cells that open and close them. Through the stomata, oxygen enters for respiration, and carbon dioxide is used for photosynthesis.

Stems: In woody plants, the lenticels on the stem's surface allow gas exchange. These are small openings that allow oxygen to pass through the bark and into the plant's tissues.

Roots absorb oxygen from the air trapped in soil particles. Root hairs are tiny extensions that help increase surface area to absorb the oxygen needed for respiration.

So, the process of respiration is essential for all living organisms, and it has evolved in many different ways depending on the species' needs and environment. From simple diffusion in sponges and jellyfish to complex systems like those in humans and birds, respiration is a vital function that supports life on Earth.

- **The structural adaptation for Circulation: Blood**

Blood plays a vital role in transporting nutrients, oxygen, and other substances throughout the body, ensuring the health and function of organs and cells. The circulatory system has evolved in different ways depending on the complexity of the organism. Here’s a simple breakdown of how blood works in various animals:

In Simple Organisms

Earthworms have red blood, which gets its colour from a substance called haemoglobin in the blood plasma. However, unlike humans, earthworms don't have red blood cells. The blood carries oxygen, nutrients, and waste products, but it’s not circulated through vessels like in humans. Earthworms have a simple circulatory system with a heart-like structure to pump blood.

Insects have haemolymph instead of blood. Haemolymph doesn’t contain red blood cells because insects don’t need red blood cells to carry oxygen. Instead, insects have a tracheal system, where oxygen diffuses directly into their tissues and cells. The haemolymph is a clear or pale-yellow fluid that carries nutrients, hormones, and immune cells, but it doesn't carry oxygen. The haemolymph circulates throughout the body cavity, bathing the organs directly.

In More Complex Organisms

Octopuses have blue blood due to a copper-based protein called hemocyanin. This binds to oxygen, but it's not as efficient as the iron-based haemoglobin in other animals.

Why Blue Blood? Hemocyanin works well for octopuses, as they have a short lifespan and don't face extreme environmental challenges like migration. The blue blood is still adequate to meet their oxygen needs.

Fish, Frogs, Snakes, Birds, and Humans: These animals have red blood cells containing haemoglobin, a protein that binds with oxygen and helps transport it efficiently through the body.

- **Cold-Blooded Animals**: Fish, frogs, and snakes are cold-blooded (ectothermic). This means their body temperature depends on the temperature of the environment. They often need external heat sources to stay warm or cold sinks to stay cool.
- **Warm-Blooded Animals**: Birds and mammals are warm-blooded (endothermic). They can regulate their body temperature internally, meaning they can stay warm even in cold environments and cool in hot conditions.

Key Differences in Blood Types

- Earthworms: Red blood (with haemoglobin) but no red blood cells.
- Insects: Haemolymph (colourless or pale yellow), does not carry oxygen.
- Octopuses: Blue blood (with hemocyanin), less efficient in oxygen transport.
- Fish, Frogs, Snakes, Birds, Humans: Red blood (with haemoglobin), efficient in oxygen transport.

So, Blood is essential for transporting oxygen, nutrients, and waste products. Its structure and function have evolved to meet the needs of different organisms. From the simple circulatory system in earthworms to the complex, oxygen-efficient blood in mammals, each system supports the survival and functionality of the organism.

- **The structural adaptation for Heart and Circulatory System**

The heart is a vital organ that pumps blood, carrying oxygen, nutrients, and waste products throughout the body. Over time, hearts have evolved differently in various species to meet their specific needs for efficient blood circulation. Let's take a look at how hearts function in different animals and how blood circulates:

In Simple Organisms

Earthworms don't have a complex heart. Instead, they have five pairs of aortic arches, which are like segmented heart parts that help pump blood throughout their body. The blood is pumped through these arches to deliver oxygen and nutrients, though it doesn't circulate through specialized vessels like in more complex animals.

Insects have a long, continuous tube-like heart located in their abdomen. It's essentially a modified blood vessel. The heart doesn't assist with gas exchange but pumps haemolymph (insect blood) to deliver nutrients to the body.

Octopus has three hearts. One heart pumps blood to the body, while the other two pump blood to the gills for oxygen exchange. This specialized system supports their complex needs and oxygen requirements.

In More Complex Animals

Fish have a two-chambered heart with a ventricle (pumps blood to the gills) and an atrium (receives oxygen-poor blood from the body). Blood circulates through the gills where it gets oxygenated before being sent to the rest of the body.

Frogs have a three-chambered heart: one ventricle (to distribute oxygen-rich blood) and two atria (one for oxygenated blood and one for deoxygenated blood). The blood mixes in the ventricle, which makes the circulation less efficient than in more advanced animals, but this is manageable because frogs have lower oxygen demands.

Reptiles (Snakes, Lizards) Like frogs, reptiles have a three-chambered heart, but with partially divided ventricles. This reduces the mixing of oxygen-rich and oxygen-poor blood. Crocodiles are an exception and have a four-chambered heart, like birds and mammals.

Birds and Mammals: Birds and mammals have a four-chambered heart: two atria and two ventricles. This separation of oxygen-rich and oxygen-poor blood allows for efficient circulation, supporting high metabolic demands. For example, birds need a large heart to provide enough oxygen for flight, while mammals rely on their hearts to regulate body temperature.

Human have a four-chambered heart with Right atrium: Receives deoxygenated blood from the body and pumps it to the right ventricle, which sends it to the lungs for oxygen. Left atrium: Receives oxygenated blood from the lungs and pumps it to the left ventricle, which circulates it to the rest of the body. The heart's design prevents oxygenated and deoxygenated blood from mixing, ensuring efficient oxygen delivery throughout the body.

Plant Circulatory System: Just like animals, plants have a vascular system to transport nutrients, water, and food throughout the plant.

Xylem and Phloem: Xylem Transports water and minerals from the roots to the rest of the plant and Phloem Transports food (sugar solution) from the leaves (where it's produced via photosynthesis) to other parts of the plant.

Water Transport in Xylem

Transpiration: Water is lost through the stomata on the leaves. This creates a suction force that pulls more water up through the xylem. Water moves up the plant due to capillary action, aided by the cohesive and adhesive properties of water.

Food Transport in Phloem

Osmosis: The process that helps move food from the leaves to other parts of the plant. Water from the xylem moves into the phloem by osmosis, carrying the sugar solution. Phloem can carry sugar in multiple directions to ensure food reaches all parts of the plant.

Different animals have evolved heart structures to meet their unique needs, from simple hearts in earthworms and insects to complex four-chambered hearts in mammals and birds for efficient blood circulation.

Plant Vascular System: Plants also have a transport system (xylem and phloem) to move water, minerals, and food throughout their body to ensure growth and survival.

In both animals and plants, the circulatory system is essential for the survival and proper function of all cells and tissues.

- **The structural adaptation for Flight**

Flying is a fascinating ability that many creatures have evolved, enabling them to pollinate, hunt, migrate long distances, and thrive in various environments. Over time, different animals have adapted their body parts into wings, which have allowed them to conquer the skies.

Evolution of Wings in Different Creatures

Insects

Evolution of Wings: Flying insects first appeared about 318 million years ago. The wings of insects are believed to have evolved from the gills found on the thorax of early aquatic insects. These gills helped with respiration in water and were also used for steering and paddling.

Adaptation for Flight: Once these insects moved to land, their gills became more suited for gliding and steering through the air. Over time, these gills evolved into wings, with size and shape adapting to the insect's needs.

- Larger Insects: Larger insects generally have stubby wings for more lift.
- Smaller Insects: Smaller insects have longer winged to be more aerodynamic.

Wing Structure: Insects typically have four wings, but some have evolved to have only two, a result of natural selection and adaptation to their environment.

Evolution from Dinosaurs: Birds are believed to have evolved from avian dinosaurs. The wings of birds are thought to have evolved from the arms of bipedal dinosaurs that were originally used for stabilizing and balancing while running.

Adaptation for Flight: Over time, these arm surfaces expanded, and eventually, they helped the birds take flight. Early birds may have used their arms to leap into the air to catch prey, a strategy that reduced competition with other animals.

Flapping Flight: As these animals flapped their wings, it helped increase their speed, eventually evolving into sustained flight. Birds are highly adapted for flight, with features like feathers that reduce air resistance.

Bats: Distinct Wing Structure: Bats are the only mammals capable of true flight. Unlike birds, bat wings are made of elongated fingers covered by a membrane of skin.

Evolution of Flight: Fossil records show that bats evolved flight after birds, around 65 million years ago. It's believed that bats first glided before evolving into flapping flight.

Adaptations for Flight: Bats have specialized features, including:

Large Heart: Bats have the largest heart relative to their body size compared to any mammal, which supports the high-energy demand of flight.

Oxygen-Rich Blood: Bats have a high concentration of red blood cells, helping them carry more oxygen for efficient flying.

Seeds in Plants

In the plant kingdom, wings are found in seeds to help them disperse over long distances, ensuring the survival of the species.

Pine Trees: Pine trees produce seeds with papery wings that allow them to be carried by the wind.

Maple Trees: Maple seeds have propeller-like wings that spin as they fall, helping them travel a greater distance.

Silk Cotton Trees: These trees have cottony seeds that are dispersed when the pod cracks open, allowing the seeds to float and spread.

Summary :-

- **Insects**: Evolved wings from gills, helping them glide and then fly. Their wings vary in size and shape based on their needs, with most insects having four wings.

- **Birds**: Evolved from dinosaurs, using their arms for balance before transitioning into flight. Their wings and feathers make them efficient fliers.
- **Bats**: Mammals with wings made of skin and elongated fingers. They have special adaptations, like a large heart and oxygen-rich blood, for efficient flight.
- **Plants**: Seed wings help plants disperse their seeds through the air, ensuring wider spread and greater survival chances.

Each of these creatures evolved unique wing structures to help them survive and thrive in their environments, whether for flight, spreading seeds, or adapting to different ecological needs.

➢ **The structural adaptation for Toxins**

Toxins are harmful substances that can cause injury, illness, or death when introduced into a living organism. Venom is a specific type of toxin, usually produced by animals to disable prey or defend against predators. Venoms are made up of proteins, enzymes, and other molecules that affect cells, tissues, and organs in different ways.

Types of Animals Venom

Snake Venom

Hemotoxin: Affects the blood. It causes red blood cells to burst and prevents blood clotting, leading to internal bleeding and organ failure. For example, rattlesnakes and copperheads have hemotoxins.

Neurotoxin: Affects the nervous system by disrupting the signals between neurons, causing paralysis. Snakes like the cobra, black mamba, and coral snake have neurotoxic venom.

Cytotoxin: Destroys body cells, causing tissue damage and organ failure. For example, gaboon vipers and spitting cobras have cytotoxins that can damage heart cells (cardiotoxic), muscle cells (myotoxic), or kidney cells (nephrotoxic).

Frogs: Some frogs, like the golden dart frog, have highly toxic skin. Their toxins, which come from their diet of ants and insects, can kill up to 10 grown men, making them one of the most venomous animals on Earth.

Scorpion venom affects muscle function. The venom contains a protein called chlorotoxin, which blocks chloride ions, leading to muscle paralysis.

Spiders: Cytotoxic venom Damages body cells and tissues, like snake venom. Neurotoxic venom Affects the nervous system, blocking signals between neurons.

Jellyfish: venom is made of porins, which form pores in cell membranes. It can cause severe reactions like rapid heart rate, cardiac arrest, difficulty breathing, and brain haemorrhaging. The box jellyfish is the most venomous creature in the world.

Plant Toxins: Since plants can't move, they've developed their own defence strategies, like thorns and spines, to protect themselves. When these fail, plants produce chemical toxins.

Cyanogenic Glycoside: Found in bamboo roots and almonds, this toxin can cause symptoms like dizziness and rapid blood pressure if consumed in large quantities. It releases cyanide, which is poisonous.

Tannins: Found in many plants, tannins give plants a bitter taste to discourage animals from eating them. They can also cause indigestion.

Furocoumarins: Released when plants are stressed or damaged. These toxins can cause skin irritation when exposed to sunlight and may also lead to gastrointestinal issues.

These toxins have evolved in various creatures and plants to help them survive, whether for hunting, self-defence, or deterring predators.

Chapter 10

Geographical Effects on Temperament

"The character of a people is shaped by the land they inhabit." — *Ibn Khaldun*

- **Since man is distinguished and separate from other beings due to his attributes such as self-reasoning and self-awareness, therefore the evidence of his courage is visible and prominent through most intelligent and courageous actions. In the prevailing treatment methods, Greek medicine relies on physical and natural principles and therefore is highly attuned and adaptive to the human temperament. Due to this balance and harmony, the changes occurring in the ecological system directly cause chaos and disturbance in the human mood and the functions that come out of it.** [(46)(54)(55)(56)]

All the world's civilizations and healing methods survive because of their uniqueness. In particular, Greek medicine is also distinguished and different from other medicines by sticking to its principles and theories. The disbelief of even one of them is a question mark on the existence and survival of Greek medicine because the role of physics in health and disease is fundamental.

We are completely surrounded by the material and non-material objects of the universe (climate, weather, houses, regions) in which the balance is not only a sign of a healthy environment but also a sign of good health for us. Any kind of change in them is not only a cause of environmental pollution but also a cause of harm and suffering for human life because they all have their own specific nature and temperament which is reflected in the secrets of human health and the effects of all these factors can be clearly seen in the human race. The reason for this is that people of different races are found on the planet and different types of plants are also found in them. [34][46]

Every species exists in equilibrium. So significant change can be seen in the functions and properties of humans belong to the planet. Human being cannot live without being affected by the mood of the place where he lives. That is why adaptation between human temperament and environmental temperament is necessary. If the human mood is in harmony with the mood of the environment, then its functions are issued correctly and health is maintained and not on the contrary, the condition is imposed, which we can observe in practical life as well. For example, where the heat is high, such as areas around the equator, people living here are more prone to skin diseases. On the contrary, joint diseases are more common in people living in colder regions. In view of these factors, physicians have increasingly shed light on the epistemic mood because of their inevitable impact on the human mood. The materials described by the ancient physicians in this chapter are scattered in the classical books of medicine. [10][11][21][46]

We are all well aware that there are different types of weather in different parts of the world, some places have almost summered all year round, some places have wintered all year round, and some places have hot weather in one part of the year and cold season in the other part of the year. These climatic and environmental changes also affect the organisms living in these places. Keeping this in mind, ancient doctors have explained the differences in the temperament of the people living in different parts of the world and have described it in detail in their writings, because Authors believed that there are many factors that affect the temperament of the people, but there are two factors that have a special effect. These include 1. Geographical variations 2. Food and drink. [29][46]

In ancient times, people had different ideas about how the Earth was divided and where people lived. They believed that there was an **imaginary circle in the sky** called the **meridian**, which was in the ninth sky. This circle stretched from **east to west** and was in the **middle of the North and South Poles**. They called it the **circle of Maadal al-Nahar (equalizer of the day)** because when the **sun reached this circle**, the **day and night became equal** in most places. On the Earth, another imaginary line was drawn, called the

Equator (Khat-e-Istawa). This line divided the Earth into two halves—the **Northern Hemisphere** and the **Southern Hemisphere**.

Ancient geographers thought that only one-fourth of the Earth was inhabited by people. They called this part **Raba Maskun**, which means **"inhabited quarter."** They also believed the Earth was round and divided it into 360 degrees. They said the inhabited part of the Earth was divided into seven regions (Aqaleem) using imaginary lines. They first divided the Earth into two halves by the Equator—the upper half was the Northern Hemisphere, and the lower half was the Southern Hemisphere.

Many old scholars thought that no people lived near the South Pole. A famous writer, **Al-Majusi**, wrote in his book **Kamil al-Sanaa** that ancient travellers never saw people living south of the equator. However, he said that if people were found there in the future, their way of life would be similar to those in the Northern Hemisphere, with only small differences. This shows that many early geographers believed that no one lived south of the equator.

There were two different groups of ancient scholars who divided the **inhabited world (Raba Maskun) into seven regions**. One group believed that people only lived up to 66 degrees north of the Equator, and the remaining 24 degrees near the North Pole were empty. They divided the first 26 degrees from the Equator into seven equal parts, which they called the seven Aqaleem (climatic regions). The first region was closest to the Equator, and the seventh region was near 26 degrees north, closer to the cold areas.

Another group of geographers also believed that people lived only up to 66 degrees north, and beyond that, the land was either empty or had very few people. They divided the area from the Equator to 66 degrees north into seven regions. However, some geographers thought that some areas near the Equator were too hot for people to live in, just like how the North Pole was too cold. They believed that the first few degrees from the Equator were too hot for life, and the North Pole was too cold for survival. This group divided the middle 50 degrees of the Northern Hemisphere into seven regions, as they believed people could only live in these areas.

Despite these beliefs, some ancient scholars thought that people also lived in the Southern Hemisphere, just like in the Northern Hemisphere. They assumed that the southern part of the world was also divided into seven regions, just like the north. But since travel was difficult in ancient times, people could not explore faraway places. Mountains, seas, and long distances made travel almost impossible. Because of this, many scholars thought that only the Northern Hemisphere had people and that the Southern Hemisphere was empty.

They also believed that three-quarters of the Northern Hemisphere was covered with water, and only one-fourth was land where people lived. This land was divided into seven regions. They studied how the sun affected different places. They believed that areas near the Equator were very hot because the sun's rays were directing all year round. But in the North Pole and surrounding areas, the sun's rays were slanted, so these places remained cold. This is why they believed that some parts of the Earth were too hot or too cold for people to live in.

These early ideas helped scholars understand the world, but today we know that people live in both the Northern and Southern Hemispheres, and climate is more complex than they thought. (5)(6)(23)(42)(55)(56)

This inhabited part was divided into seven equal parts by these people. They used to determine the mood of these continents by making the relationship between the earth and the sun as the basis. He believed that the regions around the equator are places where the sun's rays are almost straight throughout the year, while the north pole and its surrounding areas are places where the sun's rays are slanted almost throughout the year. This is the reason why it is always cold here. (55)(56)

The Earth has different climate zones because different parts of the planet receive different amounts of sunlight. At the centre of the Earth, there is an invisible line called the **Equator**, which divides the planet into two halves: the **Northern Hemisphere** and the **Southern Hemisphere**. The areas near the Equator get the most sunlight, so they are the hottest. The **Tropic of Cancer** is located **23.5 degrees north** of the Equator, and the **Tropic of Capricorn** is **23.5 degrees south** of the Equator. These two lines mark the farthest points where the sun's rays can shine directly overhead. Beyond these, there are colder areas near the **Arctic Circle**

(66.5 degrees north) and the **Antarctic Circle** (66.5 degrees south), which are close to the North and South Poles. These places remain very cold all year because they get very little direct sunlight.

The **Equator** is the hottest place on Earth because the sun shines directly over it throughout the year. Countries like **Indonesia, Brazil, and the Democratic Republic of Congo** are found in this region. The weather here is always warm and humid, with a lot of rain. Thick rainforests grow in these areas, and many animals like **jaguars, parrots, snakes, and frogs** live here. These animals have adapted to survive in hot and wet conditions. For example, **snakes and frogs can climb trees**, and **jaguars have spotted fur** that helps them blend into their surroundings. Some animals, like owls and jaguars, are **active at night** to avoid the daytime heat.

The **Tropical Zone**, which lies between the **Tropic of Cancer and the Tropic of Capricorn**, is also warm, but it can be drier in some places. Countries like **India (southern part), Thailand, Nigeria, and Venezuela** are in this zone. The temperature is high, and many different animals live here, such as **elephants, tigers, crocodiles, and monkeys**. Some animals, like **elephants, have large ears** to help them stay cool, while others, like **tigers, have strong muscles** to catch prey. **Sloths** move very slowly to save energy, and **crocodiles** spend a lot of time in water to keep cool.

The **Northern Temperate Zone**, which lies between the **Tropic of Cancer and the Arctic Circle**, has a mix of **hot summers and cold winters**. Most of the world's population lives in this area, in countries like **the USA, China, Japan, and parts of India**. This region has many different landscapes, including forests, mountains, and grasslands. Animals here, such as **bears, foxes, deer, and rabbits**, have special ways to survive changing seasons. For example, **bears hibernate** (sleep for months) in winter, and **foxes grow thick fur** in cold weather but shed it in summer.

The **Southern Temperate Zone**, located between the **Tropic of Capricorn and the Antarctic Circle**, has cooler weather because it is surrounded by oceans and mountains. Countries like **Argentina, South Africa, and New Zealand** are part of this zone. Animals here include **kangaroos, penguins, and wombats**. **Kangaroos have strong legs** to jump long distances and escape predators, while **penguins have thick feathers** to stay warm in cold waters.

The **Arctic Region**, near the **North Pole**, is extremely cold throughout the year. In this region, for **six months, the sun never rises**, and for the next **six months, it never sets**. Countries like **Canada, Russia, and Greenland** are in this area. The cold and icy conditions make survival difficult, but animals like **polar bears, Arctic foxes, and reindeer** have adapted. **Polar bears have thick fur and a layer of fat** to keep warm, **Arctic foxes change their fur colour** to blend in with the snow, and **reindeer migrate** to warmer places when food is scarce.

The **Antarctic Region**, near the **South Pole**, is even colder than the Arctic. This is because Antarctica has high mountains and thick ice sheets that trap the cold air. While the **warmest temperature recorded in the Arctic** was **+5°C**, the highest temperature ever recorded in **Antarctica was -12°C**. Only a few animals can survive here, including **penguins, seals, and krill. Penguins have thick feathers**, **seals have blubber (a layer of fat) to keep warm**, and **krill (tiny sea creatures) serve as food** for many animals.

The reason why the **polar regions** are so cold is that the sun's rays **hit them at an angle**, meaning the sunlight spreads out over a large area instead of hitting directly. Also, **snow and ice reflect sunlight**, preventing the ground from absorbing heat. Because of this, **most people prefer to live in the Northern Temperate Zone**, where the weather is neither too hot nor too cold.

By understanding these climate zones, we can learn why some places are always warm, others are freezing, and how different animals adapt to survive in their environments.

Modern geographical research tells us that India is located to the north of the equator. Its northernmost regions are known as Kashmir and Ladakh, while its southernmost point is Kanyakumari. Just below India, to the south, is Sri Lanka, and slightly below Sri Lanka, the equator passes through.

If we imagine a line at 10 degrees north of the equator, only a small part of India will fall under it. This includes regions like Kerala, parts of Tamil Nadu, and Puducherry.

Ancient scholars and geographers divided the world into different climatic zones (called *aqalim* in old terminology), based on temperature and weather conditions. According to this system, India is divided into three main climatic regions:

1. **First Region (Aqleem Awwal):** This includes southern Indian states like Kerala, Tamil Nadu, Karnataka, and the southern part of Maharashtra. These areas are closer to the equator, so they have a hot and humid climate. Like, Chennai and Kochi experience high temperatures and frequent rainfall.
2. **Second Region (Aqleem Dovom):**

This includes Maharashtra, Chhattisgarh, Odisha, Madhya Pradesh, Gujarat, Tripura, Manipur, Meghalaya, Rajasthan, and the southern part of Uttar Pradesh. These areas have a mix of hot and moderate climates. For example, cities like Mumbai and Bhopal have hot summers but also experience some monsoon rains.

3. **Third Region (Aqleem Soam):** This includes northern Rajasthan, Haryana, Delhi, Uttarakhand, Punjab, Himachal Pradesh, northern Uttar Pradesh, Jammu, and Kashmir. These areas have colder winters and moderate summers. For example, Delhi has very hot summers but also cold winters, while Kashmir experiences heavy snowfall.

If we start measuring directly from the equator instead of from 10 degrees north, the classification of regions will change. In that case, India's northernmost regions, like Jammu and Kashmir, could be placed in a fourth region (*Aqleem Chaharam*), which consists of extremely cold areas. Additionally, the **Tropic of Cancer** passes through **eight Indian states:** Gujarat, Madhya Pradesh, Rajasthan, Chhattisgarh, Jharkhand, West Bengal, Tripura, and

Mizoram. These states experience both hot summers and some cooler months depending on their location.

For example, Jaipur (Rajasthan) has very hot summers, while Shillong (Meghalaya) is cooler due to its higher altitude.

The climate of a city depends on many things like its location (latitude), the type of soil, whether it's high or low, and how close it is to rivers or mountains. It also depends on whether the air flows freely or is blocked by hills or buildings.

Scholars believe that places near the Tropic of Cancer and Tropic of Capricorn are hotter than places farther away, like near the equator or in the north. This happens because areas directly under the sun's path have moderate temperatures. They don't get extremely hot like the regions under the tropics, and they don't get very cold like the far north or south. For example, countries near the equator, like Indonesia or Brazil, have warm weather most of the year, while places farther north, like Canada or Russia, get very cold winters.

The air in such regions also stays more stable, unlike areas where the sun moves closer and farther throughout the year. Famous scholars like Ibn Sina believed this idea to be correct.

It is well known that places where the sun is directly overhead most of the time are hotter than those farther north. The sun's constant presence makes these places warmer. Even when the sun tilts slightly, it stays relatively close. Because of this, people in hot regions tend to be more active and energetic. Their bodies also adapt to the heat, so they often have darker skin and sharper senses. For example, people from Africa or South Asia usually have darker skin compared to those from colder regions like Europe.

The type of soil in a city also affects its climate:

- Rocky and mountainous areas are cold and dry, like parts of Afghanistan.
- Areas with lots of bushes and greenery are cold and moist, like some parts of England.
- Soil with clay or limestone is hot and dry, like deserts in Saudi Arabia.
- Sandy or river areas are hot and moist, like the Nile River region in Egypt.

As we know that every person's temperament is appropriate and moderate according to him, but it is definitely a little different compared to other people. Similarly, due to climatic changes, the mood of people living in one region of the world is different from the people living in another region of the world. This difference of mood can be in terms of health and disease, in terms of intellect and consciousness, in terms of the occurrence of various diseases, in terms of the skin and hair on the body, in terms of health of the organs and in terms of fat and muscle in the body. It is a fact that apart from geographical influences, terrestrial or geological factors also play a major role in the weather of any place. Apart from this, the sun's rays and solar energy reaching this part also play an important role. [11][34][54]

Now we know that the sun's rays fall in different ways in different places of the world, besides the presence or absence of mountains, different rivers, oceans and deserts etc. Also affect the weather of any region. For example, the distance of both North Pole and South Pole from the Equator is equal, so the weather of both places should be almost the same, but it is not so, the South Pole is colder than the North Pole. And the reason for this is that the North Pole is a sea area while the South Pole is a mountain area and the presence of both sea and mountain places are causes discord in the weather. According to a report, the lowest temperature ever recorded at the North Pole (-60 C) while the lowest temperature ever recorded at the South Pole (-83 C). These changes in weather not only affected different plants, but also the animals and humans found in this place are not spared from their effect. It can be easily understood through the knowledge of Biodiversity. [11][34][54]

The environment we live in has a significant impact on our body, health, and personality. Different regions, based on their temperature, humidity, altitude, and geographical features, influence how people grow, age, and behave.

Effects of Hot Regions : In hot regions, people generally have **darker skin and curly hair** due to constant exposure to the sun. Their bodies lose moisture quickly, which leads to **faster aging and early wrinkles**. Because of excessive sweating and dehydration, people in these areas tend to feel **weaker and more fearful**. For example, in **desert regions like Saudi Arabia, Sudan, and parts of India**, the intense heat makes people's bodies adapt by producing more melanin, leading to darker skin. They also tend to be more reserved and less physically strong compared to people from colder climates.

Effects of Cold Regions : People living in **cold climates** are often **stronger, more energetic, and braver**. The cold weather requires their bodies to work harder to maintain warmth, which strengthens their muscles and overall endurance. If the climate is not only cold but also **humid**, then people tend to have **well-built, muscular bodies with smooth skin**. For instance, **people from Scandinavian countries (Norway, Sweden, Finland) and Russia** are known for their **tall height, strong physiques, and endurance in harsh conditions**. Their cold environment also makes them more resistant to certain illnesses, as their immune systems are naturally stronger.

Effects of Humid Regions : In **humid (moist) areas**, people generally have **soft skin and a chubbier body** because moisture in the air prevents their bodies from drying out. However, the excessive humidity makes it harder for sweat to evaporate, which can make them feel sluggish. These places also have **moderate temperatures**, meaning summers are not too hot, and winters are not too cold. However, humid environments can lead to **chronic illnesses like fevers, diarrhea, and skin infections**. For example, in **coastal cities like Mumbai (India), Florida (USA), and Bangkok (Thailand)**, people often experience **high humidity**, making them sweat a lot and feel fatigued easily.

Effects of Dry Regions : Dry regions are known for their **rough climate**, with extremely **hot summers and freezing winters**. People living here tend to have **dry skin, rough hair, and lean bodies**. Their **brains and muscles also lack moisture**, which can make them more irritable. These areas allow heat and cold to be felt more intensely due to **the lack of moisture in the air**. For example, in **desert regions like Rajasthan (India), Arizona (USA), and parts of Iran**, people often experience **dry, cracked skin and increased thirst** due to the lack of humidity in the air.

Effects of High-Altitude Regions (Mountains) : Mountainous regions, with their **thin and clean air**, produce **strong, brave, and long-living** people. The high altitude makes their lungs and hearts work harder, making them physically tougher. For example, **Tibetan monks in the Himalayas** are known for their **strong endurance and long lifespans**, thanks to their body's adaptation to low oxygen levels. Similarly, people from **the Andes in South America** are naturally **resilient and hardworking** due to their mountain lifestyle.

Effects of Low-Lying Regions (Valleys & Plains): People living in **low-lying areas** often experience **high humidity and frequent fog**. Their water sources are usually **not very cold and may become stale if they don't flow properly**. This can lead to **higher rates of infections and respiratory diseases**. For example, in **Bangladesh, which has many low-lying regions**, frequent floods and stagnant water contribute to **health issues like malaria and waterborne diseases**.

Effects of Rocky & Open Lands: Regions that are **rocky and uncovered with snow** experience **extreme weather**—very hot in summer and freezing in winter. People from such places have **strong, muscular bodies with thick body hair** for protection against harsh weather. They are usually **aggressive, hardworking, and skilled in various professions**. For instance, **Afghan and Mongolian people** are known for their **strong warrior-like nature** due to their challenging terrain and extreme climate.

Effects of Snowy Mountain Regions: People living in **permanently snowy areas** have **similar characteristics to those in cold regions**. They are **hardy, physically strong, and adapted to freezing temperatures**. For example, **people in Siberia and northern Canada** have adapted to survive in **ice-cold weather**, developing strong bodies and a resistance to cold-related diseases.

Effects of Coastal Regions: Coastal areas have **moderate weather**—not too hot, not too cold. However, due to the **moisture from the sea, the air is usually humid**. This humidity can make people's bodies **retain more water**, leading to **weight gain and skin problems**. If coastal regions are in the **north**, they are **cool and humid**; if in the **south**, they are **warm and humid**. For example, in **Kerala (India), Greece, and Japan**, the sea breeze keeps the weather moderate, but people often face **joint pains and skin allergies** due to high humidity.

Effects of Northern Regions: Northern regions, which are generally colder, have people with **strong digestion and longer lifespans** due to their bodies generating more heat. However, **women in these regions tend to have less menstrual flow**, and some studies suggest **lower fertility rates** in extreme northern regions. For example, **in Russia and Canada**, people have **strong builds and better immunity**, but birth rates can be lower due to the harsh climate.

Effects of Southern Regions: Southern regions, which are **warmer and more humid**, tend to make people **sluggish and prone to diseases** like **asthma, epilepsy, and digestive issues**. Their bodies are often **filled with excess moisture**, making them feel **tired and weak**. For example, in **Brazil and other tropical South American regions**, **skin infections, malaria, and respiratory diseases** are more common due to the warm and wet climate.

Effects of Eastern and Western Regions: Eastern and western regions experience different effects depending on the **winds and local climate**. In some areas, **eastern winds are dry and refreshing**, while in others, they are **humid and heavy**. Similarly, **western regions** can either be **moist and thick** or **cool and dry**, depending on their location. For example, in **India, eastern winds bring rain**, while in **Arabian deserts, they bring dry heat**. In **Europe, western winds bring rain**, while in **Africa, they bring dry heat**.

So, the environment we live in plays a huge role in shaping our **bodies, health, and personalities**. Hot places make people **age faster and weaker**, while cold places make them **strong and energetic**. Humid regions cause **chubbiness and sluggishness**, while dry regions create **lean and rough-skinned people**. Mountainous areas produce **tough and long-living individuals**, while coastal regions bring **moderate climates but health issues from humidity**. Understanding these environmental effects helps people **adapt their lifestyles, diet, and healthcare choices** to stay healthy and live better.

MIZAJ-E-AQALEEM (Temperament of Regions)

- **According to Fakhruddin razi:** Mizaj of 4th Aqleem is real Motadil (optimum).
- **According to Ibn Sina:** Mizaj of nearest regions of equator is real Motadil (optimum).
- **According to Ibn Rushd:** Mizaj of 5th Aqleem is real Motadil (optimum).

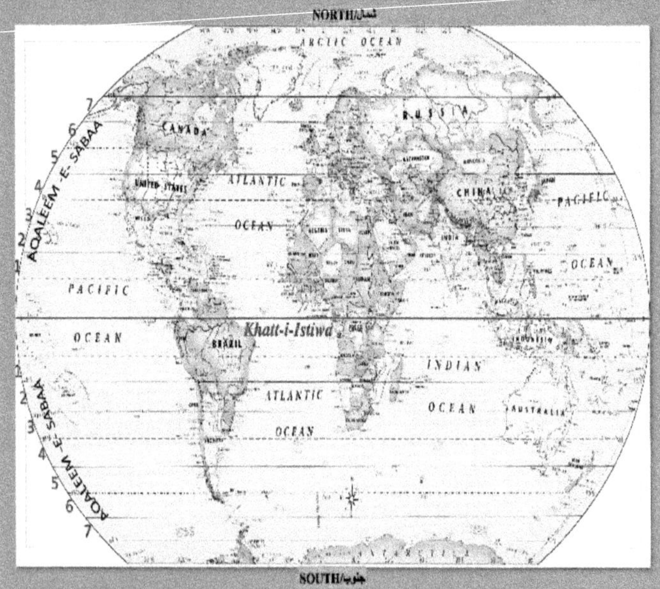

•**Northern cold zone/Arctic circle** (منطقہ باردہ شمالی): Area from خط قطب شمالی (Arctic line) to قطب شمالی (North pole)- UK, Denmark, Alaska, Poland etc. (66.5°*N to* 90°*N*).

•**Northern normal zone** (منطقہ معتدلہ شمالی). Area from خط سرطان (Tropic of cancer) to خط قطب شمالی(Arctic line) - Israel, Libya, Iraq, Iran, Pakistan, India (from Kashmir to upper part of MP) etc.(23.5°*N to* 66.5°N).

•**Tropical zone**(منطقہ حارہ): Area from خط سرطان(Tropic of Cancer) to خط جدی(Tropic of Capricorn) – India (From lower part of MP to Kanyakumari), Saudia Arabia, Oman, Kenya, Thailand, North Australia, Malaysia etc.(23.5°*N to* 23.5 °S).

•**Southern normal zone**(منطقہ معتدلہ جنوبی): Area from خط جدی (Tropic of Capricorn) to خط قطب جنوبی (Antarctic line)-Argentina, South Africa, New Zealand, Tasmania, South Australia etc. (23.5°*S to* 66.5°S).

•**Southern cold zone/Antarctic circle** (منطقہ باردہ جنوبی): from خط قطب جنوبی(Antarctic line) to قطب جنوبی (south pole) – Almost no population .(66.5°*S to* 90°S).

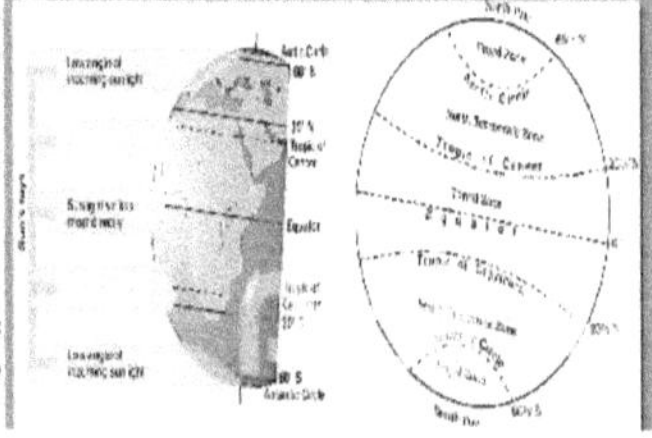

Chapter 11

Ecosystem and Biodiversity

"Nature does not hurry, yet everything is accomplished." — *Lao Tzu*

- **Gaia Theory,[10] introduced by James Lovelock, is the idea that Earth acts like a self-regulating system where living things and the environment work together to keep the planet healthy and suitable for life. Instead of thinking of Earth as just a rock with life on it, the theory suggests that all living things (plants, animals, and microorganisms) and non-living things (air, water, and soil) are interconnected and help maintain balance.**

Living things influence their surroundings in ways that make Earth a better place for life. In return, the environment supports and sustains life. This creates a cycle where life and Earth work together to maintain conditions like stable temperatures and clean air.

Examples

1. **Oxygen and Life**: Billions of years ago, tiny organisms like cyanobacteria started producing oxygen through photosynthesis. This oxygen

changed Earth's atmosphere, eventually making it possible for animals and humans to live.

2. **Plants and Carbon Dioxide**: Trees and plants absorb carbon dioxide (a greenhouse gas) and release oxygen. This helps regulate the climate by keeping temperatures stable and the air breathable.
3. **Ocean and Temperature**: Oceans absorb heat and carbon dioxide, which helps prevent the planet from becoming too hot or too cold. Tiny organisms in the ocean, like plankton, also play a role in regulating gases in the atmosphere.

The **Gaia Theory** suggests that life actively creates and maintains the conditions necessary for its survival. A good example is the stabilization of oxygen in Earth's atmosphere at about 21%. This balance is crucial because:[10]

- If oxygen dropped below 15%, fires couldn't burn, and organisms would suffocate.
- If oxygen rose above 25%, fires would ignite spontaneously, causing widespread destruction.

For millions of years, Earth's systems, influenced by life, have kept oxygen levels stable to support plants, animals, and other organisms. Over time, a protective ozone layer formed in the upper atmosphere (made from three-atom oxygen molecules), shielding life from the Sun's harmful ultraviolet rays. This protective system allowed more complex life forms, like fungi, plants, and animals, to evolve and thrive.

The Gaia Theory helps us understand how deeply connected life is with Earth's systems. For example, if humans cut down too many trees or pollute the oceans, it disrupts the natural balance and makes Earth less suitable for life. This is why protecting the environment is so important—it's like taking care of the "living system" of Earth.

In short, Gaia Theory reminds us that life and Earth work together as a team, and when one part is harmed, it affects the whole system.

The **Santiago Theory**,[10] developed by Humberto Maturana and Francisco Varela, explains that living things are defined by their ability to maintain and renew themselves, a process called **autopoiesis** (self-making). It means living organisms actively create and sustain themselves while interacting with their environment. For example, a bacterium takes in nutrients, uses them to maintain its structure, and adapts to changes to survive. Similarly, humans digest food, fight illnesses, and adapt to their surroundings to stay alive. This theory shows that life is a continuous, self-organizing process where organisms sustain themselves and adapt to their world.

It is commonly recognized that from the earth's formation millions of years ago, the environment has been changing. It took millions of years for conditions to be favourable for life to exist. Earth's early conditions were not as they are now. Early on, there were plenty of forests, lots of open space, rivers, ponds, and canals, plenty of rocks, lots of rainfall, lots of wild creatures, and a lot of other things. The people who lived in those times were also not the same as those living now. Many species of primordial atmosphere became extinct because their Temperament may have diverged greatly from the bounds of that species. As a result, new species whose Temperament was in harmony with the ambience replaced the extinct species. (9)

A person with hot and dry Temperament is not able to endure prolonged exposure to intense heat or dryness. Such environmental characteristics tend to disintegrate quwah and arwah, making it impossible for tabiyat to carry out the tasks required for survival. They also tend to affect the Temperamental attributes of the subject in an excessive way that is incompatible with survival. People who create harmony with their surroundings can survive in such unfavourable conditions. This newfound harmony with the surrounding environment would undoubtedly come with a new set of boundaries created in Temperament, and consequently, new forms and purposes. In this way, when one species goes extinct, another one arises. (46)

Every living thing undergoes Temperament alterations due to changes in its surroundings. This shift in animate bodies' Temperament might either push some of them outside the bounds of their species or race, or it could move them closer to the most appropriate Temperament. Naturally, the bodies of those animate entities whose Temperament falls within the bounds of their species or race would live, while the remainder would experience an extreme kind of Temperamental deviation to the point of being incompatible with life and, consequently, functional deviation. It is stressed that the boundaries of Temperament between species and races define the features of certain species and races (e.g., human begets human). It is the existing Temperament, which has developed throughout time as a result of interaction with the environment and numerous environmental and dietary elements that alter it to the degree required for life in that altered environment. [46]

The diet's quality with reference to Hotness and Moistness (Ruṭūbat) is the environment's most determining factor. Like all animate objects, each individual's organ is constructed from the same basic materials, but each organ has a unique appearance and function. This functional and structural variation is difficult to identify and explain in terms of genetic and molecular mechanisms.

Unani philosophers believe that each organ has its own Temperament, and hence its own structure and functions, in this context. A common Temperament cannot be shared by two organs. The same organ cannot work similarly in two people who are not of the same species or race since they cannot have a same Temperament. Because each organ has the same Temperamental limitations, structural similarities can be observed. For example, the livers of all humans are within the liver's Temperamental limitations; but, changes in the liver's Temperament within its unique boundaries in a given individual can lead to functional variances. [46]

Environment is the basic life support system that provides air, water, food and land to all living organisms.

Human life will be at risk if they don't live in harmony with the environment. Environmental problems are not limited to the local, regional and national level, but there are several global issues. Many global summits, conferences and conventions are regularly conducted by the United Nations and many steps are taken to minimize human-induced issues by signing agreements with around 150 countries. The 18th Heads of State and Government Summit of the Group of 20 (G20) will take place in September 2023 in New Delhi, India. Under the Indian Presidency, the G20 in 2023 will focus on the theme, 'One Earth, One Family, One Future'.

This year (2024), the theme of the World Environment Day says, "Land Restoration, Desertification, and Drought Resilience." It's tied in with bringing back healthy land, keeping desserts from developing, and managing water shortages. Trees, healthy soil, and clean water are imperative for a solid planet. In any ways, biodiversity is us and we are biodiversity.

There are several major environmental problems are: Deforestation, Global Warming, Climate Change, Pollution such as air, water, noise, etc., Urbanization, Fracking, Waste disposal, Decline in Wildlife Population, Loss of biodiversity, Biomagnification, Eutrophication, Ozone Layer Depletion, Acid Rain etc.[88-108.]

Deforestation: Deforestation has resulted in several ecological imbalances such as increase in temperature, deficiency in rainfall etc. It has also resulted in the extinction of several species of animals and plants. Every year 1.1 crore hectares of forests have been cut down around the world. In India alone 10 lakh hectares of forests are destroyed which has resulted in so many harmful effects. [18][19]

Deforestation has resulted in the loss of many wonderful species of plants and animals and many are on the verge of extinction. More than 80% of the world's species remain in the tropical rainforest. Reports say that about 50 - 100 species of animals are being lost each day as a result of destruction of their habitats. [18][19]

The observance of International Biodiversity Day (May 22) was yet another reminder of the pivotal role our natural world plays in resolving the climate change crisis, which, along with the decline of biodiversity, poses an existential threat to our future. Biodiversity, the rich variety of life forms and their interconnections with each other and the environment, is everywhere: inside our bodies as ubiquitous microbiomes, in our backyards, villages, towns, and cities, and in remote wild places as well-organized ecological communities and ecosystems. Maintaining and enhancing biodiversity on land and in oceans is perhaps the least expensive mechanism to sequester carbon dioxide from the atmosphere so as to cool our land and oceans. [18][19][20][57]

Mitigation of climate change is but one of the several benefits we derive from biodiversity. It also fulfils our basic needs for food, shelter, medicines, mental health, recreation, and spiritual enrichment. To face the continuing decline in the quality of our environment, we will need to rely more and more on solutions that draw upon biodiversity or nature, also called nature-based solutions to secure our future. It is biodiversity that will restore our degraded lands and polluted rivers and oceans and sustain our agriculture in the face of climate change. It is biodiversity that will form the basis of a new sustainable green economy. And it is biodiversity that will inspire our children to opt for a more humane, just, and hopeful future, which accords primacy to the living world. (57)

Despite the importance of biodiversity that ultimately sustains all human endeavors, we have been poor stewards for caring and nurturing life on earth. Globally as well as in India, we have failed to adequately conserve and manage our precious, irreplaceable natural heritage. Biodiversity is declining worldwide, and our last remaining, largely isolated ecosystems are degrading due to changes happening around them, such as loss of species, climate stressors etc. Deforestation results in many effects like floods and droughts, loss of soil fertility, air pollution, extinction of species, global warming, spread of deserts, depletion of water resource, melting of ice caps and glaciers, rise in sea level and depletion of ozone layer. [(18)(19)(57)]

February of 2024 was the hottest February ever. So was this year's January. This is in continuation of a streak, the last seven months of 2023 also marked record highs for those months. Records have been set and broken in successive years, which means that the world is heating up. Not only are temperatures rising, but they are also rising at a faster rate than ever before. The gap between the record temperatures set in 2023 and 2024 and the old records from previous years which were broken are considerably wide, showing that the rise in temperature is rapid. [58]

Global warming and Greenhouse Effects: Global warming is a complex and pressing issue that refers to the long-term increase in Earth's average temperature due to human activities, particularly the emission of greenhouse gases into the atmosphere. [18][19]

Green House Effect is a process by which radiant heat from the sun is captured by gases in the atmosphere that increase the temperature of the earth ultimately. The gases that capture heat are called Green House Gases which include carbon dioxide (CO2), methane (CH4), Nitrous Oxide (N2O) and a variety of manufactured chemicals like chlorofluorocarbon (CFC). Increase in greenhouse gases lead to irreversible changes in major ecosystems and climate patterns. For example, coral ecosystem is affected by increase in temperature, especially coral bleaching observed in Gulf of Mannar, Tamil Nadu. [18,19,98]

Human activities lead to produce the greenhouse effect by- [18][19]

- Burning fossil fuels, which releases CO2 and CH4
- Way of Agriculture and animal husbandry practices
- Electrical gadgets like refrigerator and air conditioners release chlorofluorocarbons
- The fertilizers used in Agriculture which release N2O
- The emissions from automobiles.

The increase in mean global temperature (highest in 4000 years) due to increased concentration of greenhouse gases is called global warming. One of the reasons for this is over population which creates growing need for food, fiber and fuel and considered to be the major cause of global warming. Clouds and Dust particles can also produce Green House effect. That is why clouds, dusts and humid nights are warmer than clear dust free dry nights. [(18)(19)]

Effects of Global Warming: Global warming causes climatic change, ozone layer depletion, rise in sea level and drowning of coastal inhabited land, melting of ice, etc. Rise in global temperature which causes sea levels to rise as polar ice caps and glaciers begin to melt causing submergence of many coastal cities in many parts of the world. There will be a drastic change in weather patterns bringing more floods or droughts in some areas. Biological diversity may get modified, some species ranges get redefined. Tropics and sub-tropics may face the problem of decreased food production. They are posing an even greater threat to human existence and so, man must start thinking of protecting the environment from pollution. [(18)(19)(88-108)]

So, if we don't take steps to stop global warming, the future could be very difficult. We will see more heatwaves, rising seas, stronger storms, and many other problems that could change life as we know it. But if we take action now by reducing pollution, saving energy, and protecting the environment, we can slow down global warming and help protect the Earth for future generations. The sooner we act, the better chance we have of avoiding these bad effects.

Global Warming Effects on Plants:[18,19,89,90,91,92]

- Low agricultural productivity in tropics
- Frequent heat waves (Weeds, pests, fungi need warmer temperature)
- Increase of vectors and epidemics
- Strong storms and intense flood damage
- Water crisis and decreased irrigation o Change in flowering seasons and pollinators
- Change in Species distributional ranges
- Species extinction

What happen in future: [18,19,89,90,91,92,98]

Global warming is a serious issue, but we can all make a difference. By taking small actions every day, we can reduce the effects of global warming and help protect the planet for future generations. The more we work together, the better our chances of stopping its worst impacts.

In the future, if we don't act to stop global warming, the Earth will continue to heat up, and this will lead to many big problems. Here's what might happen:

1. Hotter Temperatures

The Earth's temperature will keep rising. This means we will experience more very hot days, which can lead to heatwaves. Heatwaves make life uncomfortable and even dangerous, especially for vulnerable people like the elderly and children. Hotter temperatures can also cause more wildfires in areas where the land is dry, and these fires can destroy homes, forests, and wildlife.

2. Melting Ice and Rising Sea Levels

As the Earth heats up, ice at the North and South Poles will continue to melt. This melting causes the water to move into the oceans, causing sea levels to rise. If sea levels rise too much, coastal cities and small islands could get flooded. People who live in these areas might have to move away because their homes will be underwater or too dangerous to live in.

According to this, the holy Quran already mention in Surah Ar-Ra'd, Ayat 41 that "Do they not see that We gradually reduce their land from its borders? Allah decides—none can reverse His decision. And He is swift in reckoning."

3. More Extreme Weather

Global warming causes more unpredictable and dangerous weather. We will see stronger hurricanes, heavy rainfall, floods, droughts, and storms. These extreme weather events can damage homes, roads, and crops, making life difficult for people. Droughts can cause water shortages, and floods can destroy homes and farms. The cost to fix the damage will be huge, and it will make life harder for everyone, especially those who are already struggling.

4. Loss of Plants and Animals

As the climate changes, many animals and plants will not be able to survive. Some animals may have to move to new places, but if they can't find a new home, they might go extinct. This is bad for the environment because each plant and animal play a part in keeping nature healthy. If too many species disappear, it will upset the balance of ecosystems and hurt everyone.

5. Food and Water Shortages

Changes in the climate will make farming harder. Some places may not get enough rain to grow crops, or the temperature may be too hot to grow food. This can lead to food shortages, meaning there won't be enough food to go around. It will also affect water supplies, as droughts make rivers and lakes dry up, making clean water harder to find. This can lead to higher prices for food and water, and some people might struggle to get the basics they need.

6. Health Problems

With higher temperatures, there will be more heatwaves, which can cause heatstroke or other health problems. People with breathing issues, like asthma, will also find it harder to breathe because the air quality will get worse. As the weather changes, diseases like malaria and dengue fever could spread to new places where they didn't exist before. This will make more people sick.

7. Economic Problems

Fixing all the damage caused by global warming will cost a lot of money. Governments will have to spend money repairing homes, roads, and other infrastructure after floods, storms, or fires. Farmers may lose crops, and businesses may suffer. Poor countries will be the hardest hit because they have fewer resources to cope with the problems. This could make the gap between rich and poor countries even bigger.

8. People Moving from Their Homes

As sea levels rise and extreme weather makes some areas unliveable, many people may be forced to leave their homes. These people will become "climate refugees" and move to other places where it is safer. This can cause problems because other countries might not be prepared for such a large number of people arriving at once, and resources like food, water, and shelter may become scarce.

If we don't take steps to stop global warming, the future could be very difficult. We will see more heatwaves, rising seas, stronger storms, and many other problems that could change life as we know it. But if we take action now by reducing pollution, saving energy, and protecting the environment, we can slow down global warming and help protect the Earth for future generations. The sooner we act, the better chance we have of avoiding these bad effects.

Strategies to deal with Global Warming:

- Increasing the vegetation cover, grow more tree.
- Reducing the use of fossil fuels and greenhouse gases.
- Developing alternate renewable sources of energy.
- Minimizing uses of nitrogenous fertilizers, and aerosols.

Loss of Biodiversity[17,18,19,56,128]

We already know that biodiversity can be expressed in terms of the different levels of biological organization such as genes, species, ecosystems and landscapes. All these four forms of biodiversity can be subjected to loss, although the most easily recognizable form of loss is that of species. Since, as stated earlier, the different forms of diversity are intimately related to one another, biodiversity loss at any one level will lead to loss at other levels too. This should be kept in mind while reading this chapter. It is only for convenience that biodiversity loss is treated separately under each of the first three levels. (18)(19)

genetic diversity is analyzed at the population level. Hence loss of genetic diversity is also studied in populations. New work suggests that the extinction rates of populations of species are far higher than has been estimated for species. The annual losses of populations are around 0.8%, which is equivalent to about 1800 populations every hour. genetic diversity is important for fitness and adaptive changes. loss of genetic diversity becomes a serious matter for concern as it will affect the fitness and evolutionary adaptability of a species. (18)

Reduction in genetic diversity within populations of species may be caused by four factors, all of which are a function of genetically effective population size. These four factors are. Founder effects, Demographic bottlenecks, Genetic drift and Inbreeding depression. (18)

The loss of species is a natural process. We know from fossil and historical data that all species have a definite life span. We also know those forces that led to loss of species as well as those that allowed certain species to survive. The theoretical calculations from fossil data suggest that as much as a quarter of Earth's species become extinct each million years. The actual reasons for this loss are not known. The explanations offered thus far range from interspecific competitions, climatic changes, accumulation of deleterious genes, result of inbreeding or extraterrestrial impacts such as those of asteroids. Well over 95% of all species that have evolved on this Earth thus far have become extinct. We also know that extinct species outnumber living ones by a factor of perhaps a thousand to one. [(18)(19)]

Loss of Ecosystem Diversity may be considered as the ultimate cause for loss of both species and genetic diversities. This has been amply indicated by fossil data as well as information presently available. Both deterministic and stochastic processes, described as responsible for species extinctions, are also responsible for loss of ecosystem diversity. This section delineates the threat factors affecting ecosystems in general as well as the magnitude of loss estimated for the major ecosystems of the world and the major causes for such a loss. The various mechanisms involved in the loss of ecosystem diversity fall into five major categories. overkill, habitat destruction, impacts of introduced animals and weeds that later become invasive, pollution and secondary losses. [(18)]

Summary of Why Everything Is Different

Why Everything Is Different is an exploration of the diversity of life, its origins, evolution, and interconnectedness through multiple perspectives, including philosophy, Unani medicine, and modern science. The book examines fundamental questions about existence, life's composition, and the forces that shape living beings. Dr. Iliyas Hussain integrates ancient wisdom with contemporary scientific thought to explain why everything in nature is unique yet interdependent.

The book begins with an inquiry into the essence of life, tracing its philosophical and scientific interpretations. Life remains an enigmatic force, manifesting through biological functions but defying precise definition. Ancient and modern perspectives—from existentialism to materialism—are discussed, along with scientific theories on the origin of life, including the Big Bang, chemical evolution, and genetic inheritance. The book also presents an Unani perspective, emphasizing the role of four fundamental elements (earth, water, air, fire) in shaping living organisms.

Evolutionary principles are explored in depth, from early Greek thought to Darwin's theory of natural selection. The adaptation of life forms across geological time is examined, with an emphasis on how changes in environmental conditions influence biodiversity. Structural adaptation, genetic variation, and ecological factors contribute to the evolution of species, reinforcing the book's core theme of interconnected diversity.

A major theme of the book is the philosophy of life and death. The Unani concept of temperament (Mizāj) plays a vital role in understanding how different organisms maintain balance. The philosophy of Equitable Temperament states that harmony in the body's elements ensures good health, while imbalance leads to disease. This perspective extends beyond human health to the broader ecosystem, where equilibrium maintains biodiversity.

The book also explores the causes of existence (Asbāb-e-Wujūd), questioning why different forms of life exist and what sustains them. Various philosophical and scientific explanations—ranging from divine creation to natural selection—are presented. The text emphasizes that life is not merely a product of biological processes but is deeply embedded in a network of relationships with the environment and other living beings.

Dr. Hussain highlights the distinctiveness of life forms by categorizing nature into three major kingdoms: minerals, plants, and animals. Despite their differences, all forms of life share fundamental characteristics, making them part of an interconnected system. The Unani perspective on biodiversity examines how structural and functional differences among creatures emerge due to their elemental composition and environmental adaptations.

The book discusses the relationship between structure and function, emphasizing how organs and biological systems have evolved to meet specific survival needs. Adaptation is a continuous process, driven by environmental pressures that shape physical and behavioral traits. Examples from Unani medicine, such as the influence of temperament on human health, are used to illustrate these concepts.

Geography plays a crucial role in shaping biodiversity and temperament. The book explores how climate, topography, and ecological factors influence the evolution of species. Human temperament, for instance, is affected by environmental conditions, dietary habits, and cultural practices, reinforcing the idea that biological diversity is not random but an adaptive response to surroundings.

The final chapters delve into ecosystems and their delicate balance. Biodiversity is essential for the survival of life on Earth, as species interact in complex ways to sustain ecosystems. The book emphasizes the need to preserve natural habitats and maintain ecological harmony to prevent biodiversity loss. The interdependence of life forms demonstrates the fundamental unity underlying nature's diversity.

Why Everything Is Different offers a comprehensive exploration of life's diversity through a blend of philosophy, science, and Unani medicine. By examining the origins, evolution, and interconnectedness of all living things, the book encourages readers to appreciate the uniqueness of life while recognizing its deep interconnections. Dr. Hussain's work bridges ancient knowledge and modern discoveries, providing a holistic perspective on the forces that shape our world. The book invites readers on a journey of self-discovery and reflection, reinforcing the idea that despite differences, everything in nature is part of a beautifully interwoven system

List of Abbreviations

- Arḍ – Earth (One of the four elements)
- Mā – Water (One of the four elements)
- Nār – Fire (Unani Element)
- Hawā' – Air (One of the four elements)
- Rukn – Element (Basic components of the body and universe)
- Arwāḥ – Spirits (Vital energies in the body)
- Ashraf Mizāj – The Best of All Temperaments
- Balgham – Phlegm (One of the four humors)
- Dafi'a – Expulsion Force (Body's ability to remove waste)
- Dam – Blood (One of the four humors)
- Gharīziyya – Innate (as in innate heat or temperament)
- Hadima – Assimilation Force (Body's ability to process nutrients)
- Kayfiyāt – Qualities (Hot, cold, wet, dry)
- Harārat – Heat (A key quality in Unani medicine)
- Ruṭūbat – Moisture (A key quality in Unani medicine
- Yubūsat – Dryness (A key quality in Unani medicine)
- Ilm-e-Hifz-e-Sehat – Science of Hygiene (Preventive medicine)
- Ilm-e-Ilaj – Science of Treatment (Therapeutics)
- Jamida – Solid Matter (One of the states of matter)
- Jadhiba – Attraction Force (Body's ability to absorb nutrients)
- Laṭīf Akhlāṭ – Subtle Humors (Refined essence of humors)
- Masika – Retention Force (Body's ability to hold nutrients)

- Mizāj – Temperament (The balance of qualities in the body)
- Mizāj Mu'tadil – Balanced/ Ideal Temperament
- Mizāj Mu'tadil Shakhsi – Most Equable Individual Temperament
- Mizāj Mu'tadil Sinfi – Most Equable Racial Temperament
- Mizāj Mu'tadil 'Uḍwī – Most Equable Organ Temperament
- Mizāj Mu'tadil Naw'ī – Most Equable Species Temperament
- Nāriyya – Fire Essence (Unani concept of fire-based qualities)
- Quwwat-e-Ḥaiwāniya – Vital Power (Animal spirit)
- Quwwat-e-Nafsāniya – Psychic Power (Mental and emotional force)
- Quwwat-e-Ṭabiyya – Natural Power (Body's inherent regulatory force)
- Quwwat-i-Muwallida – Reproductive Faculty (Ability to reproduce)
- Ṭabī'at – Nature (The body's natural balance)
- Ustuqussāt – Primary Components (Unani term for basic elements)
- BC – Before Christ
- CO_2 – Carbon Dioxide
- CaO – Calcium Oxide
- ATP – Adenosine Triphosphate
- CRISPR – Clustered Regularly Interspaced Short Palindromic Repeats

- DNA – Deoxyribonucleic Acid
- H_2O – Water (Dihydrogen Monoxide)
- J/g°C – Joules per gram per degree Celsius (Specific Heat Capacity)
- RNA – Ribonucleic Acid
- UNANI – Unan (Greek) Traditional Medicine System
- Ṣūrat Naw'iyya - Specific For atomic structure.

Index

Bibliography

1. **Avicenna.** *The Canon of Medicine. Translated by Gruner OC, Shah MH. Karachi: Rafi Publication; 1999.*
2. **Zaidi IH.** *A textbook of Kulliyat-e-Umoor-e-Tabi'yah. 1st ed. Aligarh: Litho Offset Printers Achal Tal; 2011. p. 1-4, 21-31.*
3. **Masihi AS.** *Kitab-ul-Miah. Translated by CCRUM. Vol. 1. New Delhi: CCRUM; 2008. p. 36, 15, 101.*
4. **Kabeeruddin M.** *Kitabul Akhlat. New Delhi: Central Council for Research in Unani Medicine; 2009. p. 37.*
5. **Jamaluddin.** *Al Aqsarai. Lucknow: Mataba Munshi Naval Kishor; Year Not Mentioned (YNM). p. 1-10, 15-25, 38, 48, 186-187, 250.*
6. **Kabiruddin M.** *Ifada-e-Kabir. New Delhi: National Council for Promotion of Urdu Language; 2001. p. 9-16.*
7. **Russell B.** *A history of Western philosophy. New York: Simon & Schuster; 1945. p. 204-207.*
8. **Razi ABM.** *Kitab-ul-Murshid. Translated by Raziul Islam Nadvi. 1st ed. New Delhi: Taraqqi Urdu Bureau; 2000. p. 2-6.*
9. **Zulkifle M.** *Origin of life in Unani perspective. J Res Unani Med. 2013;2(2):52-57.*
10. **Capra F.** *The web of life. London: Flamingo; 1997. p. 215-221, 228, 303-304.*
11. **Darwin C.** *On the origin of species. Delhi reprint 2023. First published in 1859. p. 25-47, 60, 141, 216, 235, 266, 414, 474.*
12. **Schrödinger E.** *What is life? Delhi: Cambridge University Press; 1944. p. 102-112.*
13. **Nizami U.** *Risala Chahar Muqala. Meer Kudratullah Karimi Press; 1930. p. 9-22.*

14. **Rabban-Al-Tabri.** *Firdausul Hikmat. Translated by Hakeem Mohd Awwal Shah Sambhali. New Delhi: Idara Kitab us Shifa; 2010. p. 20-40, 57.*
15. **Abubakar M.** *Estimation of the Ajza-e-Mohallila as a determinant of Moistness (Ruṭūbat) in Three Vital Organs of Animals [dissertation]. Bengaluru (IND): Rajiv Gandhi University of Health Sciences; 2016.*
16. **Furley D.** *The Greek cosmologist. Vol. 1. London: Cambridge University Press; 1987. p. 16, 20, 79.*
17. **Rahman A, Aslam M.** *The Unani concept of temperament (Mizāj) and its correlation with biodiversity in present epoch - A review. Int J Sci Res. 2013.*
18. **Krishnamurthy KV.** *An advance book of biodiversity principles and practice. New Delhi: CBS Publishers & Distributors; 2022. p. 1-5, 10, 20-38, 81-95.*
19. **Navaneethan S.** *Environment, biodiversity, and disaster management. Chennai: Tamizhi Books; 2022. p. 52-87, 106-114, 146.*
20. **Antonelli A.** *The hidden universe. UK: Ebury Publishing House; 2022. p. 2, 20-25, 40, 89, 97, 110.*
21. **Mathurana HR, Varela FJ.** *Tree of knowledge. Boston: Shambhala Publications; 1992. p. 39, 70, 95, 102, 115, 124.*
22. **Ibn Sina.** *Kulliyat-e-Qanoon. Translated by Kabiruddin HM. 2nd ed. New Delhi: Idara Kitab ul Shifa; 2015. p. 20-35.*
23. **Majusi AIA.** *Kamil Al-Sana'a. Translated by Hakeem Ghulam Hasnain Kantoori. Vol. 1. New Delhi: Idara Kitabus Shifa; 2010. p. 19-28.*
24. **Nafis B.** *Kulliyat-e-Nafisi. Translated by Kabiruddin H. New Delhi: Idara Kitab us Shifa; 1954. p. 12-42, 59, 148-149, 215, 220.*

25. **Zaidi IH, Zulkifle M, Ahmad SN.** *Temperamentology: A scientific appraisal of human temperament. Aligarh: Competent Xerox Centre; 1999. p. 1-9, 12-17.*
26. **Galen.** *Work on human nature. Translated by Singer P. Cambridge: Cambridge University Press; 2018.*
27. **Belo C.** *Chance and determinism in Avicenna and Averroes. Boston: Brill; 2007.*
28. **Mukhtar S.** *Arastu Hayat wa Talimat Fikar wa Falsafa. Lahore: Shahid Publishers & Booksellers; Year Not Mentioned (YNM).*
29. **Ibn Rushd AW.** *Kitab ul Kulliyat. Urdu translation. Lahore: Maktaba Daniyal; 2017. p. 33, 38, 48, 49, 64, 68, 77, 216, 243.*
30. **Ahmad N, Ahmad W, Zulkifle M, Khan TN.** *Surat, Mizaj aur quwa ke mabain talluk aur tabiyat-e-mudabbira badan. Tarjuman-e-Tibb. July-Dec. Bangalore; 2015. p. 44-50.*
31. **Zulkifle M, Baig DMF.** *Itlaqi Kulliyat. Bangalore: National Institute of Unani Medicine, Empire Printers; 2023. p. 42, 62-64.*
32. **Atkin P, Paula JD.** *Atkin's physical chemistry. 9th ed. Oxford: Oxford University Press; 2010. p. 2-5.*
33. **Jalinus.** *Kitab Fil Mizaj. Translated by Rahman HSZ. Aligarh: Ibn Sina Academy; 2008. p. 102-118.*
34. **Arzani A.** *Mufarreh ul Quloob. New Delhi: Idara Kitab us Shifa; 2002.*
35. **Jeans J.** *The mysterious universe. England: Penguin Books; 1930. p. 57-61.*
36. **Khan HMA.** *Muheet-e-Azam. New Delhi: CCRUM; 2012.*
37. **Qaiser KM, Chaudhary AA.** *Surat Nauiya: A modern-day concept in Unani classics - an analytical description. J Res Unani Med. 2016;5(2):39-41.*
38. **Tabri M.** *Moalijat-e-Buqratiya. Translated by CCRUM. Vols. 1-3. New Delhi: CCRUM; 1995.*

39. **Jalinus.** Kitab-Fil-Anasir. Translated by Rahman HSZ. Aligarh: Ibn Sina Academy; 2008. p. 10-17, 72, 87-100.
40. **Jurjani I.** Zakhira Khwarizam Shahi. Translated by HH Khan. Vol. 1. New Delhi: Idara Kitabul Shifa; 2010.
41. **Azmi AA.** Basic concepts of Unani medicine: A critical study. 1st ed. New Delhi: Jamia Hamdard; 1995.
42. **Azmi HAA.** Mabadiyat-e-Tibb par ek tahqeeqi nazar. New Delhi: Taraqqi Urdu Bureau; 1991.
43. **Ahmed SI.** Kulliyat Asri. 1st ed. Delhi: New Public Press; 1983.
44. **Baig MF.** Importance of dominant Rukn in determination of Masakin in Unani perspective [dissertation]. Bengaluru (IND): Rajiv Gandhi University of Health Sciences; 2019.
45. **Ahmed SI.** Introduction to Al-Umoor Al-Tabiyah. New Delhi: CCRUM; 1980.
46. **Zaidi IH, Zulkifle M, Ahmad SN.** Temperamentology: A scientific appraisal of human temperament. Aligarh: Competent Xerox Centre; 1999. p. 1-9, 12-17.
47. **Zulkifle M.** Mizaj: concept and insight. J Res Unani Med. 2015;4(1):24-33.
48. **Ibn Sina ASAR.** Al Qanoon Fit Tibb. Translated by Hakeem Ghulam Hasnain Kantoori. New Delhi: Idara Kitab ul Shifa.
49. **Aristotle.** Generation of animals. London: William Heinemann Ltd; Cambridge: Harvard University Press; 1914. p. 211, 255.
50. **Aristotle.** Parts of animals. Cambridge: Harvard University Press; 1961. p. 55, 289, 367.
51. **Aristotle.** History of animals. London: George Bell & Sons, York Street, Covent Garden; 1883. p. 27.
52. **Grant V.** The origin of adaptations. New York: Columbia University Press; 1963.
53. **Yagil R.** The desert camel: Comparative physiological adaptation. 1985.

54. **Khan TN, Itrat M.** *Kitabul Mizaj. New Delhi: Hidayat Publishers and Distributors; 2023.*

55. **Ali M.** *Mizaj-e-Insani Aqleemi Tanazur Main. Aligarh: Universal Book House; Year Not Mentioned (YNM).*

56. **Bawa K.** *Biodiversity is us and we are biodiversity. Bangalore City Edition, The Hindu. June 2022.*

57. **The Hindu Data Team.** *2024 records hottest ever January and February. Bangalore City Edition, The Hindu. March 2024.*

58. **Aristotle.** *De Anima. Translated by Hamlyn DW. Books II & III. Oxford: Clarendon Press; 2002.*

59. **Siddiqui MA.** *Importance of Arkan in continuation of life [dissertation]. Bengaluru (IND): Rajiv Gandhi University of Health Sciences; 2019.*

60. **Sartre JP.** *Being and nothingness. Translated by Barnes HE. London: Routledge; 2003.*

61. **Frankl** *VE. Man's search for meaning. Translated by Lasch I. Boston: Beacon Press; 2006.*

62. **Aristotle**. *Nicomachean ethics. Translated by Ross WD. Oxford: Oxford University Press; 2009.*

63. **Seneca**. *On the shortness of life. Translated by Costa CV. London: Penguin Books; 2004.*

64. **Heidegger** *M. Being and time. Translated by Macquarrie J, Robinson E. Oxford: Blackwell Publishing; 1962.*

65. **Husserl E.** *Ideas: General introduction to pure phenomenology. Translated by Gibson WR. London: George Allen & Unwin; 1931.*

66. **Heidegger M.** *Being and time. Translated by Macquarrie J, Robinson E. Oxford: Blackwell Publishing; 1962.*

67. **Merleau-Ponty M.** *Phenomenology of perception. Translated by Smith C. London: Routledge & Kegan Paul; 1962.*

68. **Laozi.** *The Tao Te Ching. Translated by Mitchell S. New York: HarperCollins; 1988.*

69. ***Vyasa.*** *The Bhagavad Gita. Translated by Easwaran E. London: Penguin Books; 2007.*
70. ***Buddhist Texts.*** *The Dhammapada. Translated by Buddharakkhita A. Kandy: Buddhist Publication Society; 1985.*
71. ***Dawkins R.*** *The selfish gene. Oxford: Oxford University Press; 2006.*
72. ***Krauss LM.*** *A universe from nothing. New York: Free Press; 2012.*
73. ***Dawkins R.*** *The blind watchmaker. New York: Norton & Company; 1986.*
74. ***The Bible.*** *New International Version. Grand Rapids: Zondervan; 2011.*
75. ***The Quran.*** *Translated by Abdel Haleem M. Oxford: Oxford University Press; 2004.*
76. ***The Upanishads.*** *Translated by Eknath E. London: Penguin Books; 2007.*
77. ***Wills C, Bada J.*** *The spark of life: Darwin and the primeval soup. Oxford: Oxford University Press; 2001.*
78. ***Hazen RM.*** *Genesis: The scientific quest for life's origin. Washington: Joseph Henry Press; 2005.*
79. ***Mesler B, Cleaves HJ.*** *A brief history of creation: Science and the search for the origin of life. New York: Norton & Company; 2016.*
80. ***Schopf JW.*** *Life's origin: The beginnings of biological evolution. Berkeley: University of California Press; 2002.*
81. ***Gold T.*** *The deep hot biosphere: The myth of fossil fuels. New York: Copernicus Books; 1999.*
82. ***Luisi PL.*** *The emergence of life: From chemical origins to synthetic biology. Cambridge: Cambridge University Press; 2006.*
83. ***Darling D.*** *Life everywhere: The maverick science of astrobiology. New York: Basic Books; 2001.*
84. ***Klyce B.*** *Panspermia: The extraterrestrial hypothesis and the origins of life. London: Cosmology Science Publishers; 2015.*

85. **Gesteland RF, Cech TR, Atkins JF.** *The RNA world: The nature of modern RNA suggests a prebiotic RNA world. Cold Spring Harbor: Cold Spring Harbor Laboratory Press; 2006.*
86. **Cairns-Smith AG.** *Genetic takeover and the mineral origins of life. Cambridge: Cambridge University Press; 1982.*
87. **Cairns-Smith AG.** *Seven clues to the origin of life: A scientific detective story. Cambridge: Cambridge University Press; 1993.*
88. **Kolbert E.** *Field notes from a catastrophe: Man, nature, and climate change. New York: Bloomsbury Publishing; 2006.*
89. **Gore A.** *An inconvenient truth: The planetary emergency of global warming and what we can do about it. New York: Rodale Books; 2006.*
90. **Lynas M.** *Six degrees: Our future on a hotter planet. London: Fourth Estate; 2007.*
91. **Henson R.** *The rough guide to climate change. 3rd ed. London: Rough Guides; 2011.*
92. **Maslin M.** *Climate change: A very short introduction. Oxford: Oxford University Press; 2021.*
93. **Archer D.** *The long thaw: How humans are changing the next 100,000 years of Earth's climate. Princeton: Princeton University Press; 2009.*
94. **Mann ME.** *The hockey stick and the climate wars: Dispatches from the front lines. New York: Columbia University Press; 2012.*
95. **McGuire B.** *Global catastrophes: A very short introduction. Oxford: Oxford University Press; 2002.*
96. **Flannery T.** *The weather makers: How man is changing the climate and what it means for life on Earth. Melbourne: Text Publishing; 2005.*
97. **Goodall C.** *How to live a low-carbon life: The individual's guide to stopping climate change. London: Routledge; 2010.*

98. **Hawken P.** Drawdown: The most comprehensive plan ever proposed to reverse global warming. New York: Penguin Books; 2017.
99. **Brown LR.** Plan B 4.0: Mobilizing to save civilization. New York: Earth Policy Institute; 2009.
100. **Bierbaum RM, Fay M.** Shock waves: Managing the impacts of climate change on poverty. Washington, DC: World Bank Group; 2016.
101. **Speth JG.** The bridge at the edge of the world: Capitalism, the environment, and crossing from crisis to sustainability. New Haven: Yale University Press; 2008.
102. **Boyle G.** Renewable energy: Power for a sustainable future. 3rd ed. Oxford: Oxford University Press; 2012.
103. **MacKay DJC.** Sustainable energy – Without the hot air. Cambridge: UIT Cambridge Ltd; 2009.
104. **Jacobson MZ.** 100% Clean, renewable energy and storage for everything. Cambridge: Cambridge University Press; 2020.
105. **Smil V.** Energy and civilization: A history. Cambridge: MIT Press; 2017.
106. **Klein N.** This changes everything: Capitalism vs. the climate. New York: Simon & Schuster; 2014.
107. **Campbell NA, Reece JB.** Biology. 10th ed. San Francisco: Pearson Benjamin Cummings; 2014. p. 120-135.
108. **Alberts B, Johnson A, Lewis J, Raff M, Roberts K, Walter P.** Molecular biology of the cell. 6th ed. New York: Garland Science; 2014. p. 250-265.
109. **Hoagland M, Dodson B.** The way life works. New York: Times Books; 1995. p. 45-62.
110. **Chaplin M.** Water: Its importance to life. Boca Raton: CRC Press; 2001. p. 10-28.
111. **Sandars NK.** The Epic of Gilgamesh. London: Penguin Classics; 1972. p. 1-30.

112.**Cohen M.** *Longevity: The science of staying young. New York: Oxford University Press; 2008. p. 45-78.*

113.**De Grey A, Rae M.** *Ending aging: The rejuvenation breakthroughs that could reverse human aging in our lifetime. New York: St. Martin's Press; 2007. p. 12-38.*

114.**Kastenbaum R.** *The psychology of death. 4th ed. New York: Springer Publishing; 2007. p. 80-120.*

115.**Jorjani J.** *World state of emergency. London: Arktos Media; 2017. p. 60-90.*

116.**Land MF, Nilsson DE.** *Animal eyes. 2nd ed. Oxford: Oxford University Press; 2012. p. 50-75.*

117.**Kardong KV.** *Vertebrates: Comparative anatomy, function, evolution. 7th ed. New York: McGraw-Hill; 2018. p. 200-250.*

118.**Epherd GM.** *Neurogastronomy: How the brain creates flavor and why it matters. New York: Columbia University Press; 2012. p. 30-55.*

119.**Vogel S.** *Comparative biomechanics: Life's physical world. 2nd ed. Princeton: Princeton University Press; 2013. p. 150-180.*

120.**Campbell NA, Reece JB, Urry LA, Cain ML, Wasserman SA, Minorsky PV, Jackson RB.** *Biology. 11th ed. New York: Pearson; 2017. p. 550-580.*

121.**Randall D, Burggren W, French K.** *Eckert animal physiology: Mechanisms and adaptations. 5th ed. New York: W.H. Freeman; 2002. p. 320-355.*

122.**Alexander DE.** *On the wing: Insects, pterosaurs, birds, bats and the evolution of animal flight. New York: Oxford University Press; 2015. p. 50-80.*

123.**Whiting MJ, Gopalakrishnakone P, editors.** *Handbook of venoms and toxins of reptiles. Boca Raton: CRC Press; 2010. p. 120-160.*

124.**Jurmain R, Kilgore L, Trevathan W, Ciochon RL.** *Introduction to physical anthropology. 15th ed. Boston: Cengage Learning; 2018. p. 100-15*

125. ***Halliday D, Resnick R, Walker J.*** *Fundamentals of physics. 10th ed. New York: John Wiley & Sons; 2013. p. 300-350.*

126. ***Chandrasekhar S.*** *The mathematical theory of black holes. Oxford: Oxford University Press; 1998. p. 120-180.*

127. ***Ashby MF.*** *Materials selection in mechanical design. 5th ed. Oxford: Butterworth-Heinemann; 2016. p. 75-130.*

128. ***Eldredge N.*** *Life on Earth: An Encyclopaedia of Biodiversity, Ecology, and Evolution. Vol. 1. Santa Barbara (CA): ABC-CLIO; 2002.*

129. ***Qarshi HMH.*** *Jame-ul-Hikmat. New Delhi: Idara Kitabus Shifa; 2011.*

130. *Zhmud L. The Origin of the History of Science in Classical Antiquity New York: Walter de Gruyter; 2006.*

131. *Brack A. The Molecular Origins of Life London: Cambridge University Press; 1998.*

132. *Seth miller. The elements as an archetype of transformation: an exploration of earth, water, air, and fire. John F. Kennedy university.2008*

133. ***Hall JE, Hall ME.*** *Guyton and Hall Textbook of Medical Physiology. 14th ed. Philadelphia: Elsevier; 2020.*

134. ***Campbell MK, Farrell SO.*** *Biochemistry. 5th ed. Boston: Cengage Learning; 2005.*

135. ***Harari YN. Sapiens: a brief history of humankind.*** *New York: Harper; 2015*

"When a person realizes he knows nothing, his questions become answers, and ignorance turns to wisdom. The infinite cannot be grasped, only believed. This is the ultimate truth."

— Dr. Iliyas Hussain

www.ingramcontent.com/pod-product-compliance
Lightning Source LLC
LaVergne TN
LVHW021136160826
845679LV00023B/1925

* 9 7 9 8 8 9 7 2 4 8 5 3 7 *